Practical Storytelling

I0102101

Practical Storytelling
By Dominic R. Villari

Published by
Rhapado Publishing
www.rhapadopublishing.com

ISBN: 978-0-9814940-2-9

About the Author

Dominic R. Villari was born in Riverside, New Jersey in 1971. He studied communications and multimedia at Rider College and Boston University. In these formidable years he was heavily influenced by the writing of South American magical realists such as Gabriel Garcia Marquez and Jorge Borges. After earning a masters degree, Dominic spent several years as an instructional designer. He has also worked as a graphic designer and interactive developer. Throughout his eclectic career and interests he has always remained a storyteller. After specializing in non-fiction writing for several years, in 2007 Dominic returned to the magical realist genre with his new novel the Ginger Bread Man.

Preface

The concept of using storytelling in personal and business applications is not new. The idea of using stories in our daily lives is embedded into the human condition. People are instinctively drawn to hearing stories and telling stories. This is certainly not the first book on storytelling or even the first book on storytelling in business and other situations.

However, many of the books on storytelling concentrate on making the case for using stories in business and everyday situations. As the title implies, this book takes a more practical approach to storytelling. The book focuses on the physical and mental aspects of how and why stories work. Building on this foundation it provides models and processes to help you improve your own storytelling ability.

The example stories presented here, including the central story: Tan's Tile were chosen specifically to demonstrate aspects of these models and processes. The result serves as both textbook and "fieldbook." The lessons in this book are accompanied by a series of worksheets located in the back of the book and downloadable at www.practicalstorytelling.com.

It is not my intention to sell additional books, seminars, videos or consulting. After reading this book you should be able to use stories for practical purposes within business and personal relationships.

Dominic Villari

Table of Contents

13. Finding Stories
Introduction | Collecting Stories | Matching Stories to Themes | Story Sources | Diversion: What Isn't a Story | 7 Secrets | Exercises

14. Putting it All Together
Key Steps | Worksheets | Getting Started | Diversion: Storyteller's Block | 7 Secrets | Exercises

15. Delivering Stories
Verbal Stories | Written Stories | Diversion: Simple Mediation | 7 Secrets | Exercises

Appendixes

Appendix A – Select Glossary

Appendix B – Sample Stories

Appendix C – Exercise Answers

Appendix D – Worksheets
Story Planning Worksheet | Audience Analysis Worksheet | Story Type Worksheet | Story Design Worksheet | Acts and Scenes Worksheet | Character Development Worksheet | Brainstorming Guide

Overview

This book examines the impact and importance of storytelling in our world, focusing on the practical application of this art within your personal and business relationships. It reviews the background and skills needed to construct a persuasive story in training, sales or marketing.

It includes worksheets to help you develop a theme and plan a story. It also explains how and why stories attract attention, achieve retention and increase the chance you'll affect behavior. This book introduces the BEARS technique of audience analysis and how to apply it by choosing a story type.

Objectives:

After reading this book you will be able to:

- Define the three cognitive challenges in conveying information.
- Construct concise story themes.
- Define the five main story components.
- Perform basic audience analysis using the BEARS technique.
- Choose a story type based on audience analysis.

The example projects and worksheets from this book are available at:

www.practicalstorytelling.com

Part I: Story Mechanics

Chapter 1: Practical Storytelling

Chapter Objectives:

1. Tell a story with the theme of creative thinking.

2. Describe Tangram, the Chinese puzzle used as a learning metaphor within this book.

Chapter Overview:

In this chapter you'll hear a story based on an ancient Chinese puzzle. We'll use this story throughout the book as a metaphor for creative thought and to illustrate storytelling technique.

Tan's Tile – A Tale of Creative Thought

One spring day Emperor Tan was building a new tile pathway through his garden. Tan admired the perfectly square shape of the clay tiles as he placed them uniformly along the path.

The last of the clay tiles slipped from Tan's hand and fell to the ground, breaking the hard-packed stone into seven pieces. The square was gone and his path would be one tile short.

"Now it will never line up," said Tan. He decided to try putting the pieces back together. After several attempts he stepped back to look at his work.

"That's a lovely swan," admired his wife as she passed by Tan in the garden.

"It's supposed to be a square," muttered Tan, returning to work.

Seeing his father's next attempt, Tan's son observed: "I saw a fox like that in the garden."

"Still not much of a square," replied Tan. He looked towards the edge of the garden, where the clay-baking ovens sat cold. It would take hours to reheat the ovens and bake a new tile.

Tan continued working with the pieces of his broken tile. Later, Tan's daughter sat beside him and watched his progress.

"Father made a kitty," declared his daughter clapping her hands. Tan let out a long sigh.

"Let us go inside and get something to eat," said Tan. He took his daughter's hand and led her back into the house.

After his meal Tan returned to the garden. He began to re-arrange the pieces again. As the sun approached the horizon, Tan stepped back from his work. The square had returned.

"Finally, the square!" proclaimed Tan. He looked around the garden for his family. "I solved the puzzle," he said to the setting sun.

But no one noticed...

About Tangram

Tan's tale is an original story featuring Tangram, an ancient Chinese puzzle. The puzzle consists of a box divided into mathematical shapes. You can form the shapes into a number of different animals, people and other objects. The exact history of the puzzle is not known, but it has been played as a game for thousands of years. It also continues to be the inspiration for stories and educational lessons. Tangram is a metaphor and exercise for storytelling because it demonstrates creative thought.

Like the Tangram, stories are made up of several unique components that can be assembled in a number of ways to deliver an infinite number of messages. In the story above, Tan wanted to re-create the original square tile. However, his family saw animals in the tile pieces. Different audiences interpret stories in different ways. Later in this book we'll explore the BEARS method of audience analysis and how it relates to story development.

Caught up in the quest for his square, Tan failed to see the creative potential in the tile pieces. He was, quite literally, unable to think "outside the box." Every time he arranged the pieces in a unique way, he immediately attracted the attention of a member of his family. However, when he finally recreated the square, no one took notice – not even the sun. There was nothing inherently unique about the square; it was the same as all the other clay tiles on the path.

Tan's tale is a metaphor for creative thought. It demonstrates how uncommon patterns can attract the attention of others. Words are like the tiles in Tan's tale. When arranged into different shapes or patterns, they catch our attention. Stories are like the animal shapes, except that we use words instead of tile pieces. In the next few chapters, we'll take a closer look at why stories like Tan's Tale capture our attention and how they help us retain information. We'll also look at how they help affect behavior. Then we'll examine story components in more detail.

Role of Storytelling

The art of storytelling has been an integral part of human culture for literally thousands of years. Ancient tribes left cave paintings that essentially tell us stories about their lives. Many of these paintings depict the hunt, the quest for food. Over the centuries humans gradually became better and better at providing for their basic needs such as food and water. This allowed us to expand our storytelling.

Stories told of cultural histories, such as the flood story common to many ancient civilizations. Parables taught values and ideas. Epics entertained people with stories of great deeds – some real, some imagined. Humans have long been masters of the metaphor, the art of using seemingly unrelated concepts to relay a specific point. This is storytelling and it is still very practical and very relevant to every day life.

Think about the most persuasive people you know in your personal and occupational life. Chances are they use storytelling to achieve their goals. They tell about humorous encounters to entertain us or relate an experience with a past client to sign a new one. Storytelling resonates with something deep inside us and speaks to the core of what it means to be human.

Chances are good that you already tell stories. However, you can harness the power of storytelling to achieve even more success in your personal and business relationships. Stories allow us to make more personal and lasting connections with the people in our lives. They help us maintain current friendships and establish new ones. Shared stories are an integral part of strong marriages and partnerships.

Storytelling also has practical application to almost every aspect of business and career. "Water cooler talk" helps us connect with our colleagues. Tales of past experience illustrate a company's mission and values. A well formed testimonial sells a product. An experience with a difficult client teaches new employees how to handle a tough situation.

How Stories Motivate

Why does an experience with a difficult client teach new employees how to handle a tough situation? Wouldn't it be easier to just give them a list of things to say?

Motivation is one of the toughest barriers in a training situation. Employees are "required" to take most courses, based on job necessity or compliance or to achieve advancement. This is a natural extension of our educational system. We attend grade school to move on to high school, high school to get into college and college to move on to a good career, and so on. Thus, we see most training programs as an obligation, something we must "get through."

Ironically, humans have a passion for learning. This is evidenced by the proliferation of education channels and programming on television. Topics on these shows are increasingly growing in sophistication. After gritting our teeth through a day of corporate training, people return home to watch a documentary about the movement of tectonic plates or the construction of the Hoover dam.

Why are we motivated to watch these programs? We watch these programs because they do not so much seek to "teach" as to tell the "story" of a particular topic. They contain acts, scenes, central characters and through lines.

For example, the first act of a documentary on dinosaurs may open on a scene in ancient Arizona, sixty-five million years ago. A herd of stegosaurus (our central characters) wanders along a dry creek bed. The herd comes to this creek during the dry season, where they can usually find water. However, this year is dryer than usual, and the herd must find water by digging into the ground (our through line).

The scene above is more interesting than an archeologist holding a leg bone in his lab. I've also conveyed several pieces of information: 1) There were dinosaurs in the area now known as Arizona sixty-five million years ago; 2) Stegosaurus traveled in herds; and 3) Dinosaurs sometimes looked for water by digging.

This technique need not involve expensive computer animation and high priced narrators, either. Documentary filmmaking has used storytelling cost effectively for years. Panning or zooming the camera along a painting or still picture with narration and music is a powerful way to tell a story. Entire Civil War and World War II documentaries have been filmed using one or two large illustrations. A powerful yet underused method in multimedia is sound and fading stills.

Storytelling can be applied to all training programs and informational multimedia. We tap into the oral traditions humans have used to communicate for thousands of years using stories, metaphors and examples. In this section we focused on training. However the same principles apply to sales, marketing and other key aspects of business.

Which of the following examples do you find more compelling:

1. An unseen narrator explains each of the safety features of a car. As the narrator reviews each feature, we see a picture of it and bullet point summarizing its importance.
2. A woman explains how a car's safety features saved the life of her and her family, followed by video of the car's crash test and shots of the cabin still intact.

The second example immediately captures our attention and seems much more personal. It taps into our experiences, needs and fears. It actually tells the story of the car. Before beginning any business project, first ask: "What is the story?"

Story Types

Not every story begins "once upon a time" or features an animated character. The first question is "what's the story?" The second is "what type of story is appropriate?" There are many story types. The key is choosing the genre that best fits your goals and personality. Stories range along three main dimensions: formality, length and complexity. The topic provides several clues and correlations to determine these dimensions.

Formality is derived from the topic and audience. Topics such as "Effective Presentations" and "Effective Writing" can be told in less formal stories, such as the comic strip characters used in the sample series. Other subjects like a medical system or company history require a more formal story. To see the book's example, visit practicalstorytelling.com.

We must also account for the tolerance of the audience. Certain groups may be less receptive of an informal story. A scenario-based program is an example of a more formal storytelling technique. In a scenario the participant is given a role within a reality-based story.

The amount of material determines length. The simplest of the three dimensions, length is determined by dividing and sub-dividing a program into groups of three to five complete bits of information, each definable in an action-oriented sentence sometimes referred to as an "objective." However not all story types are sustainable over certain lengths. Stories perform most effectively and efficiently when used consistently.

Complexity is the most difficult dimension to calculate and deal with, especially in longer stories. More complex topics generally require more complex stories. The story in a complex program anchors the material in metaphor and example. This helps the user visualize the material. In other cases the story is a simple one. A series of concise and practical worksheets may be the whole narrative.

A good example of this technique is the book *What Color is Your Parachute* by Richard Nelson Bolles. The reader is an active participant in the book, which utilizes a series of questions and worksheets to help someone discover his or her true calling.

In this case the audience themselves are the main characters and the plot is the task at hand. Animated characters or comics don't help in this case. Just as a story must resolve itself, the learner must complete a specific sequence of events to resolve the task at hand.

The storytelling technique is a unique approach to design, not a way to trivialize the topic. There are different types of stories, ranging from lighthearted character treatments to "real life" scenarios. Analysis of the topic, audience and organizational personality inspires the appropriate story. Later sections of this book examine each of these aspects as well as story types in greater detail.

Cost-effective Storytelling

At first glance storytelling may seem expensive. The History Channel and Discover Channel now favor sophisticated computer animation and re-creations over the simple picture panning method described earlier. If you look close though, you'll still see some of the earlier techniques applied to the technology. For example, it's common to create one computer model of ancient city and use several "fly-by" shots from different angles.

There are several methods to make storytelling cost-effective. Educational storytelling has roots in documentary, a genre of filmmaking with traditionally small budgets. Below are several additional methods that provide powerful storytelling while reducing costs:

- **Live storytelling.** Don't underestimate the power of someone simply telling a story. Word of mouth is still the most powerful motivator in most forms of advertising.

- **Sound and stills.** An underused method in multimedia is sound and fading stills. A developer's first instinct is often to use video. However, a series of stills that fade into each other with a sound or voice track can be just as effective. It's cheaper and uses less bandwidth.
- **Re-use.** Often elements of a program can be used multiple times in subtly different ways. With modifications, the same script can be used in a workbook, job aid and online training tool. Pictures and video can also be re-used in different ways (such as the documentary example above).
- **Cloning.** One of the benefits the computer offers is cloning and modification of objects. You can create an element once as a template, then modify it slightly for a multitude of uses.
- **Alternative animation.** Animated characters have become increasingly more fluid in their movements. However, a little movement goes a long way. In fact, limited movement sometimes becomes "stylistic." A classic example of this minimalist animation is Terry Gilliam's work on "Monty Python's Flying Circus." A more contemporary example is the animation style used by DNA Productions in "Olive, the Other Reindeer."
- **Economy of scale.** Design methods become more efficient when they are used repeatedly. Steps in creation can be streamlined, and lessons learned applied to future projects.

A constant within all of these methods is a need for good writing. The underlying text, whether it physically appears in the program or is read in the background, carries the through line. Even the most expensive animation cannot cover up bad writing. With good writing and creative methods storytelling can be both interesting and cost-effective.

Applying Stories

The Practical Art of Storytelling refers to the use of stories to enhance our every day lives by establishing deeper connections with other people. These deeper connections can lead to a number of benefits in both our personal lives and our careers.

This book is divided into three main parts. In Part I: The Mechanics of Stories, we'll continue to explore the underlying reasons why stories impact our lives and the lives of others. An awareness of these concepts is the first step to employing stories on a more practical level.

In Part 2: The Anatomy of a Story, we'll break down stories and storytelling into a series of inter-related parts. Once you understand all the parts, you'll be able to construct stories specifically suited to your individual goals. All of the worksheets included in this section are also available at practicalstorytelling.com.

In Part 3: Practical Application of the Story, we'll review the use of stories in everyday life through a series of sample stories. These example stories cover a range of different goals, both personal and business. All of the examples in this section are also available at practicalstorytelling.com.

Each chapter of the book is divided into several main sections. The title page of each chapter includes several learning objectives and an overview of the chapter. Following the actual content of the chapter are three additional elements:

- **Diversion** – a light and interesting story or activity related to the chapter.
- **7 Secrets** – seven key points from within the chapter.
- **Exercises** – short series of fill in the blank questions to test your retention and several discussion questions to get you thinking.

Although this book contains a certain amount of theory and background, the main focus is on the actual application of storytelling. The content and worksheets are designed to help you practice the art of storytelling in your everyday life. If have any questions or comments during or after reading the book, please visit practicalstorytelling.com or email me at this address: ask@practicalstorytelling.com.

Diversion: Make your own Tangram

It's relatively easy to make your own Tangram. Use the pattern at www.practicalstorytelling.com to cut shapes out of cardboard, foam or heavy paper. It's more interesting to make the shapes different colors.

Once you've cut out the pieces, see how many different animals you can create. Pick your five favorites and try to write a simple story around them. Next, see if you can use that story or a similar one together with Tangram for your next training, sales or marketing program.

7 Secrets

- Be careful when carrying clay tile pieces.
- It's hard to reproduce a perfect square.
- People notice unusual patterns.
- Typical patterns, such as a square, often go unnoticed.
- Uncommon patterns attract attention in words as well as tile pieces.
- Creative thought captures attention.
- Stories come in a variety of different types and styles, applicable to many different situations.

Exercises

Fill in the Blanks

1. Tan's Tile is based on an ancient Chinese puzzle called
_____.

Discussion Questions

1. Why does Tan's family notice the animal shapes, but not the square?

2. In what ways can you use the Tangram puzzle to stimulate creative thought in your organization?

3. What types of stories are applicable to your everyday life?

Chapter 2: Attract Attention

Chapter Objectives:

- List the three cognitive challenges stories overcome.
- Describe how Tan's Tile meets the challenge of attracting attention.
- Explain why uncommon patterns attract our attention.

Chapter Overview

This chapter examines the way Tan's Tile attracts attention and explains the reasons behind our perception of pattern and changes in pattern.

Cognitive challenges

In Chapter 1 we saw that storytelling overcomes two main cognitive challenges:

1. **Attract attention** – Tan's family was immediately drawn to the unique shapes he created. Hopefully the opening story also attracted your attention to the book.
2. **Achieve retention** – Tan's family remembers the specific shapes, they probably don't remember the square. Hopefully the opening story has provided you with a memorable metaphor for creative thought.

In this chapter we're going to add a third:

3. **Affect behavior** - The goal of any training, marketing or sales program is to initiate or modify behavior. The objective of a training program is to teach skills or knowledge that directs behavior. The objective of a sales or marketing program is get someone to purchase or purchase more of a product or service.

Whether you're trying to sell a car or just make a new friend you have to overcome each of these three cognitive challenges. Within this chapter and the next two chapters we'll examine how storytelling overcomes each of these challenges in more detail.

How Stories Attract Attention

Tan's tile is a simple square before it breaks. Although the tile no doubt represented quality and craftsmanship, it was one among the many throughout the emperor's palace. The moment the tile slid from Tan's fingers though, it became something more. Split into pieces, the tile could be reassembled into a number of different forms.

As Tan is rearranging the pieces, his wife notices a swan, his son a fox, and his daughter a cat. The animal shapes attract attention because they represent uncommon patterns among the other square tiles. We practice the same basic concept when we use bold type or bullet points.

We see by the refraction of light. It enters our eye through the cornea and is projected onto the retina. The retina contains cells called rods and cones that help us detect a range of colors. We see various "objects" based on color differences. For example:

ATTRACT ATTENTION
ACHIEVE RETENTION
AFFECT BEHAVIOR

The words you see on this page are a function of the contrast between the blackness of the letters and the whiteness of the page. That's why print is harder to read when it's smaller or lighter in color. It's harder for our eyes to detect the contrast. Conversely, we see things more clear when there is greater **contrast** between the colors. We see the word "contrast" in the previous sentence better because it's larger and darker.

Similarly, repeated contours tend to blur together in our vision, while opposing contours stand out. Can you look at the following line and immediately tell how many times the letter "X" appears -- just by looking and not by specifically counting?

XXXXXXXXXXXXXXXXXXXXXXXXXXXXXXXXXXXXXXXXX

Now look at this line:

XXXXXXXXXOXXXXXXXXXOXXXXXXXXXXXOXXXX

How many times does the letter "O" appear? You see the precise number of O's almost immediately because they stand out against the existing pattern of X's.
Let's look at another example:

XXXXXXXOXXXXXXXXXXXXXXXXXXXXXOXXXXXXX
XXXXXXXOXXXXXXXXXXXXXXXXXXXXXOXXXXXXX
XBXXXXXXXOXXXXXXXXXXXXXXXXXXXOXXXXXX
XXXXXXXXXOXXXXXXXXXXXXXXXXXXXOXXXXBXX

How many O's could you see this time? How about the number of B's? The human eye can perceive patterns on a sophisticated level. This allows us to effectively process the incredible amount of input we receive.

Up to this point, we've only looked at physical examples. But we perceive mental patterns as well. This occurs as the brain processes the information it receives from the eye. If you see the four-line pattern above again, you'll probably experience a sense of familiarity, even if you don't remember exactly where you saw it.

After we've seen a cat and associated the word "cat" with it, we know that animal to be a "cat" when we see it again. In fact, our mind's application of that pattern is so sophisticated that we can see almost any breed of cat and still know it's a cat.

Even that isn't the amazing part. We can see the pattern even in an abstract collection of shapes. Like Tan's daughter, we can recognize the form of a cat even if it's constructed from Tangram pieces, just as Tan's daughter did in the story. In fact, we don't even have to see the whole pattern to recognize it. Can you recognize just the eye of a cat when you see it? For a demonstration of these concepts, visit www.practicalstorytelling.com and click on the "patterns" link.

Putting Patterns to Work

But why spend all this time on patterns? By understanding how patterns are formed and processed, we become better able to manipulate them to deliver our message. For example: What do you think of as a classified ad? Probably something like this:

Improve your sales, marketing and training products. Meet learning objectives by telling stories. We can teach you how. For more information, visit practicalstorytelling.com.

The ad above uses action words such as "improve" and "meet." It is written in active voice and even implies a direct benefit. However, chances are good this ad would not attract attention. The problem is that it fits right into the pattern of most classified ads. It would blend in with all the others on the page.

Classified ads are an example of a complex pattern. We expect them to look a certain way. Try the following experiment: look through the classified section of your favorite periodical. When you stare at the pages as a whole, how many of the ads actually catch your attention? The ones that do are probably boxed or contain a picture. Everything else tends to blur together.

That's our brain interpreting the overall pattern of the pages. Now pick a couple of pages and read line by line through each ad. Did you notice any products or services you're interested in? That's why some people make a point to read every ad in the classified section of their favorite periodical (especially if it's hobby-related).

Even if you read the ad above though, you probably won't remember it. Aside from the use of action words and the implication of a benefit, it's not that memorable. Most of the ads probably employ both of these techniques. Now look at the following classified ad:

Henry Ford has a problem. It takes a mechanic a day to build one car. To get ideas, Ford tours a meat packing plant. At the plant, meat travels on hooks. At each station a worker makes a different cut. Ford's idea for the automobile assembly line is born. He moves the cars through the factory and each worker builds one part. Ford solves his business problem by looking at an industry parallel yet different to his own. For more stories, visit practicalstorytelling.com.

The story in this ad breaks the usual pattern, just as the tile animals break the pattern and capture the attention of Tan's family. It attracts attention and stands out among the usual classified ads.

The examples we've looked at so far involve the direct use of individual stories. However, as we continue in this book, we'll also be looking at ways to use the qualities of storytelling to convey information.

Not Just Gimmicks

Effective stories are well thought out and tightly constructed. If you own a restaurant that sells chicken sandwiches, just putting a guy out front in a chicken suit is not a story. Consider Chik-fil-A's long running "cow campaign." Cows appear on billboards and posters holding the message: "Eat Mor Chikin." (The misspellings are intentional.)

The cow itself doesn't attract attention. Unless you're a dairy farmer, cows aren't all that exciting. This campaign is successful because it's based on the story of a bunch of cows who want people to eat chicken (rather than the cows). The cow is actually the central character, not the story itself. The cow's quest to not get eaten is the plot.

Although this advertising seems gimmicky at first glance, it's actually well planned. Here are just some of the choices that were made:

- The use of "life-like" cows to enhance the absurdity
- The crooked writing and misspelling for comedic effect
- The misspelling of "chikin" mirrors the spelling in the brand name
- The cows write on a simple whitewashed board with black paint

These are just few of the important choices that were made when this story was constructed. This campaign contains a number of successful story elements such as humor. The fact that the words are crooked and misspelled is part of the appeal. We've probably never seen a cow write, but if they did we just assume they wouldn't be able to spell. The notion the cows can write at all is actually "suspension of disbelief" another bonus you get when telling stories.

Another key point is that we identify with the cow. "How do we identify with the cow?" you ask. Think about it: would you want to be eaten? Imagine there was a popular restaurant selling Solient Green (as Charlton Heston pointed out in the campy science fiction film by the same name: "Solient Green is people! It's people!"). You'd probably be writing signs about eating more vegetables in your diet.

Identifying with the Characters

The interesting thing about identification is it usually occurs on a deeper level than we realize. In fact, it works best when we identify without even realizing it. We identify with the cows out of our innate need for survival. We root for the cows without even realizing why.

Abraham Maslow, one of the founders of humanistic psychology, describes five levels of human needs. Chances are you learned about Maslow in school, but classified him as one of those "areas you don't use in real life." However, when applied to a specific situation, Maslow's Hierarchy actually suggests practical strategies.

Maslow's theory was that we climb these needs like a ladder; we must fulfill the lower or "basic" needs before we can achieve the higher ones.

1. **Physiological** – Food, water, air and shelter.
2. **Safety** – Security and stability.

3. **Love and belonging** – Social needs and acceptance.
4. **Esteem** – Pride in one's self.
5. **Self-actualization** – Be the best person you can be.

Consider that participants approach a training program, advertising campaign, presentation or meeting with a finite supply of personal energy. Activity at each of Maslow's levels of need draws off some of this energy. For example if you're giving a presentation and the room is too hot or too cold, a certain portion of the participant's energy is devoted to that condition.

Remember the last time you were in a situation where the temperature did not suit you? We maintain constant awareness of a temperature that is just a few degrees beyond our acceptable range. Although our mind is still able to pursue other activities, a portion of our mental energy is siphoned off in the awareness of the uncomfortable temperature.

In the example above we are identifying with the cows on the lowest rung of the ladder: survival, the basic need for life. The second rung, safety is also a connection. It seems silly to think of yourself identifying with a cow, but just by giving the cow slightly human nuances makes it work.

We can address the need for safety in a meeting by fostering an atmosphere in which questions and suggestions are welcome. Group exercises and icebreakers build up a common bond among the participants.

We can build esteem by encouraging participant contributions to discussion. Fulfillment of learning objectives or achievement of a meeting goal can be considered limited self-actualization. Maslow's hierarchy becomes a tool through which we can address the individual needs of others. Connecting with basic needs allows us to attract attention.

Diversion: Your Hierarchy of Needs

This chapter introduced Maslow's Hierarchy of Needs and provided a practical example of the hierarchy in real life. What main points are included on your Hierarchy of Needs? Take a few moments to consider each level and envision the practical application of each to you.

1. Physiological
- Do you eat to live or live to eat?
- Do you have favorite foods or no preference?
- Are you a collector or do you travel light?
- Is home where you hang your hat or something more permanent?

2. Safety – Security and stability.
- Do you deadbolt the doors or leave the screen door open?
- Do you feel secure around others or are you self-reliant?
- Are you a planner or more spontaneous?
- Do you have a regular routine or prefer every day to be different?

3. Love and belonging – Social needs and acceptance.
- How important are your relationships to your identity?
- Are you close to your family?
- How large is your circle of friends?
- Are you a social butterfly or more comfortable at home?

4. Esteem – Pride in one's self.
- Do you like yourself?
- How would you describe yourself?
- How satisfied are you?
- What do you consider your major accomplishments?

5. Self-actualization – Be the best person you can be.
- What do you need to be happy?
- Are you defined by your accomplishments or your personality?
- How do you define yourself?
- What makes you happy?

7 Secrets

- We physically see by refracting light.
- When interpreting light, the human brain looks for patterns.
- The human brain interprets patterns on many levels.
- We can identify abstract as well as detailed patterns.
- The human brain compares patterns to existing memory for identification.
- Uncommon patterns attract attention.
- We can take advantage of the way in which the mind sees patterns.

Exercises

Fill in the Blanks

1. When delivering a message, you face the following three cognitive challenges:

a. _____

b. _____

c. _____

2. We physically see by refracting _____.

3. This occurs in the eyes through _____ and _____.

4. We see objects more clearly when there is _____ between the colors.

5. Tan's family notices the animal shapes as opposed to the square shape because they represent _____ _____.

Discussion Questions

1. What are some additional abstract and/or sophisticated patterns we are able to interpret (such as the Tangram cat shape)?

2. Do your current training, sales or marketing programs use common or uncommon patterns? What are some strategies for using uncommon patterns in future programs?

3. Which has more impact: black and white or color? Is this true in all situations?

Chapter 3: Achieve Retention

Chapter Objectives:

- Describe how Tan's Tile achieves retention by helping the reader retain its main ideas.
- Explain how short-term and long-term memory allows us to remember information.

Chapter Overview:

This chapter examines the mental processes behind our retention of the key points in stories like Tan's Tile. We'll explore the differences between short-term and long-term memory and establish why we need to get our messages into long-term memory. The chapter also covers techniques for moving information into long-term memory.

Association and Long-term Memory

Let's return to the story of Emperor Tan for a moment. Imagine the scene at dinner later that evening. Tan no doubt announces the successful re-creation of his square tile. However, all his family can talk about are the wonderful animals he was able to create. Perhaps if Tan gives it some thought, he'll realize that the square, because it follows common patterns, simply isn't as memorable.

This is a biological offshoot of the same science that attracted our attention in the first place. In order to register an uncommon or unknown pattern, our mind focuses more attention on it. This allows us to recognize the pattern the next time we see it. A cat holds more fascination for you the first time you see one. That feeling of interest is our brain's way of requesting more information about the object.

We have a natural desire to register the pattern for future reference.

At the dinner table, Tan's family talks about his tile animals because at that point they still reside in their short-term memory. However, what about breakfast the next morning? Any guess about who might still remember the animals?

Depending on how interesting or unusual the occurrence was, they might all remember. However, there is one person in the family who is more likely to remember one of the tile animals than the rest. Tan's son associates the arrangement of the tiles with a fox he's seen in the garden. The association helps him remember.

Once you attract attention, it's relatively easy to get into short-term memory. Short-term memory is electrical. It's actually an extension of sight itself. After our eye refracts the light, that information is passed along the optic nerve directly into the brain. In a fraction of a second, our brain compares this electrical impulse against the records in long-term memory. It's in this instant the brain discovers that the pattern is unique.

The unique pattern gives us a "one day pass" so to speak, into the brain. That electrical memory remains until we go to sleep. Have you ever woken up in the middle of the night with a great idea or the memory of a vivid dream? No matter how hard you try, it's usually difficult to remember these things once we wake up. This is a demonstration of short-term memory cleaning itself out.

By contrast, long-term memory is designed to last years or even a lifetime. This is the land of Abraham Maslow and his Hierarchy of Needs. Here we store all the information we need for survival, relationships, fulfillment, etc. That's why we have natural desire to learn about the cat the first time we see it.

Because it has to last for future reference, long-term memory is chemically based. Chemical reactions in the brain form lasting patterns that we can recognize throughout our life. Our brain uses these patterns to interpret what we see.

The keys to staying in long-term memory are pattern and association. This is somewhat ironic because we had to use uncommon patterns to get noticed in the first place.

However, it is logical. We're interested in the cat the first time we see it because we want to be able to recognize it again. That's why it's important to nest patterns within the story. In Tan's Tile, the animal shapes are patterns that represent creative thought while the square pattern represents the opposite.

Association is a well-known trick for remembering. If you've ever studied music, chances are you know the meaning of "every good boy does fine" and "FACE." This phrase and word are acronyms used for reading the notes on sheet music. Music itself is another association device. If you recognize the phrase "stronger than dirt," chances are good you know the musical note that goes with each word (either from the commercial or the Doors song).

Other associations are visual or verbal cues such as the one Tan's son uses to connect the broken tiles with the fox he saw in the garden. So if we have all these methods already, why do we need stories?

Stories inherently apply all of these methods and allow you to subtly weave them around your message. The Tangram fox and the fox in the garden in Tan's Tile represent an association. Just as Tan's son associations the tile shapes with the fox he saw in the garden, you can associate that example with this chapter.

The entire story of Tan's Tile demonstrates the use of creative thought and storytelling, as well as being an example of it. I can also draw from the story to provide repetition of the main points without boring you by simply stating the same thing over and over again. The story helps me re-present the ideas in different ways.

Metaphor and Example

Two effective ways of emphasizing key points in your message are metaphor and example. An illustration of metaphor is the way the shapes in the Tangram are used to represent the components of a story. The shapes are easier to remember. However, if the audience remembers the shapes, they are better able to remember the concepts associated with them. Specific examples are another method of establishing long-term memories.

The Tangram is a metaphor, but examples often work just as well. If you think about the years of history class you've had, you may not remember many of the specific dates, but you most likely remember specific occurrences such as the Boston Tea Party. By remembering the Boston Tea Party, you also remember the colonies were protesting taxes (tea = tax in long-term memory). That's why the Boston Tea Party was an effective strategy by the rebels – not only did it send a key message to Parliament, it was memorable.

The Spanish-American War was largely fought on the back of the slogan: "Remember the Maine." The Maine was an American battleship sunk off the coast of Cuba. The initial conclusion was that the Spanish had blown up the warship. (Actual investigations have been inconclusive.) Nonetheless, "Remember the Maine" became a rallying cry for the war.

In this case alliteration does the heavy lifting. "Remember the Maine" contains several "m" sounds that make it chemically easy to remember. Another example is the "Battle of Bunker Hill." History indicates it's easier to go to war if you have a good slogan.

Finding a Connection

The trick to turning a simple suggestion, idea or persuasion into a story is to find a connection. Don't just explain to a colleague why something is a good or bad idea. Tell an actual account of when that idea was tried. Let the outcome demonstrate your point for you. Don't just walk up to someone you want to meet and remark that the room is crowded - give an example of how crowded.

It seems a bit unnatural at first because we tend to think of stories as "mini-events." A friend tells us about her trip. We sit down to watch our favorite program. We read a book about John Adams. With practice, we can make stories a more integrated aspect of our lives.

The connection is the extended pass that gets us into long-term memory. Remember: the barrier to short-term memory is deceptively simple. All we have to do is break the pattern a bit. The guy in the chicken suit can do that much. Chances are we won't remember him a mile up the road, though. To get into long-term memory we need to build a connection such as the one with the cows.

Before you can establish a connection, you need to examine your core message:

- "I make a strong contribution and deserve a raise."
- "We have the best solution for your business."
- "You're an interesting person and I'd like to spend more time with you."

Once you've determined your core message, or "theme" it's easy to see a natural connection:

- "I've made some innovations to the new product line…"
- "Last year we had a client with exactly your problem…"
- "Remember that night we were talking and walked right past your house…"

All of the examples deal with one type of story: an "account." An account is a simple retelling of a true occurrence or incident. There may be slight embellishment or certain aspects of story may receive more emphasis than others. However, the core of the anecdote is usually true (or at least true as we see it).

Anecdotes are generally the easiest type of story to use. We all have anecdotes. Just about anything that happens to us during the day is a potential anecdote. (Some are just more interesting than others.) Any trip to the bank can be an anecdote. However, a trip in which there's no line but the teller still makes us walk through the rope maze is a much more interesting one.

Anecdotes are also very flexible. We can emphasize or de-emphasize different aspects of an anecdote based on our audience or purpose. If we're trying to entertain, we may play up the more humorous aspects of the anecdote. For example, we could describe in more detail all the turns in the maze at the bank or how we tripped over a pole at one point.

If we're using the same anecdote as a simple way to illustrate inefficiency we stick close to the main points and emphasis how much longer it took than usual. This type of modification works well with just about any anecdote. Anecdotes are a good way to get started in practical storytelling. This book examines other story types in more detail in a later chapter of the book.

Diversion: Watch Some TV

There are a lot of good examples of storytelling on television. However, the ones most relevant to practical storytelling are up in the "higher" numbers of the cable guide. Those of you who are "infotainment" junkies know exactly what I'm talking about: Discovery, Discovery Health, History Channel, History Channel International, National Geographic, etc. The documentary programming on these channels makes excellent use of storytelling to make dry topics more interesting.

Watch these programs and pay careful attention to the way they are constructed and filmed. You should be able to pick up at least one to three techniques or strategies from each program. Look for the following:

- How does the program initially attract your attention?
- How is the plot organized?
- Who are the main characters in the story and how are they developed?
- What types of visual aids are used (stills, computer graphics, etc.)?
- How does the program end off before each commercial break?

7 Secrets

- Short-term memory is electrical.
- Short-term memory is cleaned out each night when we sleep.
- Long-term memory is chemical.
- Our messages must pass to long–term memory for retention.
- Long-term memory uses patterns and association.
- Develop metaphorical connections between your story and the information in your message.
- Stories make repetition easier.

Exercises

Fill in the Blanks

1. The member of Tan's family most likely to remember their animal shape is Tan's _____.

2. Short-term memory is _____-based.

3. Long-term memory is _____-based.

4. For our messages to survive, they must get into _____ _____.

5. The keys to staying in long-term memory are _____ and _____.

Discussion Questions

1. What associations help you remember facts and skills?

2. Using the information about long-term memory, what are some strategies for making repetition more affective?

3. How can the method used for attracting attention be leveraged when moving information into long-term memory?

Chapter 4: Affect Behavior

Chapter Objectives:

- Define the process of affecting behavior.
- Explain why stories like Tan's Tile have the potential to affect behavior.
- List the three benefits stories add to your ability to affect behavior.

Chapter Overview:

In this chapter we'll explore the deeper challenge of affecting behavior. We'll examine the meaning of affecting behavior and explore the three benefits storytelling provides for this activity.

Actions, Conditions and Standards

Affecting behavior is probably the hardest of the three challenges you encounter when delivering training, sales or marketing messages. However, if you've attracted attention and achieved retention, you're at least halfway there. First, let's take a look at what is meant by "affect behavior."

Affect behavior: To initiate a new behavior or modify an existing behavior based on a specific business message.

In order to affect behavior you must clearly state the specific behavior you want to initiate or change. In training, behavioral results are usually expressed in "learning objectives." However, an objective is also an effective way to express an intended sales or marketing result. For our purposes, we'll also refer to "affect behavior" as a noun, synonymous with the term "objective" defined below.

To be useful objectives must be measurable. A measurable objective has three main components:

- Actions
- Conditions
- Standards

Actions

Take a look at the learning objectives at the beginning of each chapter in this book. Each begins with an action verb such as "explain," "list" or "define." Avoid vague or passive verbs such as "understand" and "know." These are immeasurable goals both in training and sales and marketing. Their exact definition is subjective.

What does it mean if we say we want the customer to "understand the benefits of our product?" Now suppose we state the following: "The customer will be able to list the benefits of our product." That's a much stronger and more measurable objective. Either the customer will be able to list the benefits of the product or they won't.

Conditions

List the conditions or pre-requisites required before the affect behavior can occur. For example, a standard condition in training is: "after completing this book." This condition is usually applied to every learning objective. In sales or marketing, a typical condition might be "after reading our corporate brochure" or "after a personal call."

Standards

Qualify your objectives with standards. Standards provide specifics about the behavior. For example: After completing this book you will be able to analyze your intended audience using the BEARS Audience Analysis Worksheet.

Standards help you set more realistic goals and make them more precisely measurable. In sales and marketing standards often include totals or percentages. For example: After receiving a personal phone call, a perspective client will visit our online catalog at least twice and purchase at least $30 worth of merchandise within one month.

It's clear how the addition of these conditions make the objective more precise. The more precise the objective, the easier it is to measure.

Behavior and the Story

Generally, the affect behavior influences the scope, length and complexity of the story. The more complicated the behavior, the more sophisticated the story must be. Every story has a sustainability limit. The sustainability limit is the amount of information or content the story can be used to transmit before the story is no longer affective.

Think of a story as a fresh piece of sandpaper. As you use sandpaper to file down a piece of wood, it gradually becomes less affective because the grain of the paper wears smooth. The longer you have to use a story in a program, the more it "wears out." After awhile, the story's patterns become too common. It becomes like the O's in the type pattern in a previous chapter.

Just as there are different grains of sandpaper, there are different densities of stories. Higher grain sandpapers can file deeper cuts in the wood before wearing out. If the wood you need to sand has several layers of varnish or is rough, you'll need a higher-grade paper. Complicated behaviors require denser, or more complex stories.

Another method is to use multiple stories, metaphors and examples, just as you can use multiple pieces of sandpaper on a hard piece of wood. To illustrate, consider the cat example and the fox examples used previously. They take some of the pressure off the main story. When using multiple stories, always tie them together.

I could have used any animal in chapter two's pattern example. I specifically picked the cat because it was one of the animals in the Tan story. The trick is to establish subtle overlap throughout the story and between your stories. This is also why you'll see me bring up earlier examples again.

This book is an example of a complex affect behavior. It requires a number of different stories that have been woven together, in addition to the "core" story of Tan's Tile and its associated Tangram metaphor. Without those common links this book would just be series of passages on different topics within storytelling.

Tan's Tile is designed to be a story about storytelling. The theme of the story contains the affect behavior: the art of telling stories. Right now you're probably saying: "That just sounds like circular logic to me."

So let's look at a couple of more practical (and less existential) examples. Let's revisit our example about the car with safety features (there's that repetition again, by the way):

- A woman explaining how a car's safety features saved the life of her and her child, followed by video of the car's crash test and shots of the cabin still intact.

We decided this approach was more interesting than simply listing and showing the car's various safety features. The core story here is an account in which this particular car saved this woman her child's lives. The affect behavior is to get the consumer to buy the car for the same reason.

To make this marketing campaign work, we need to link the story to the affect behavior. It's not enough to just tell the story. We need to express her decision to buy the car for the safety features:

"I choose the K5000 because I wanted the safest car for my child. It turned out it was also the safest car for me. We were driving home on a rainy night when a truck pulled out in front of me..."

You can probably imagine the rest of this story. That shared experience is part of what makes this story work. We've all driven home on a rainy night; we've all had trucks pull out in front of us. Equally important is the affect behavior is right in the first sentence of the story: "I choose the K5000." That's exactly what we want the listener to do (and the reason we want them to do it – safety).

Let's look at another example. A parent is trying to convince a child seeing a certain movie will probably give them nightmares. One method might be for the parent to tell a story about when he or she was young. Perhaps they ignored the advice of their parents and ended up with nightmares for a week.

Influence of Stories on Behavior

Stories almost always attract attention. More often than not, they'll also achieve retention if properly constructed with metaphor and example. Both of these assumptions are founded in the biological science behind sight and memory. However, human behavior and its motivations are unpredictable. The best we can do is to increase the odds in our favor.

Stories can't guarantee a behavioral change in the same way they can almost guarantee attention and retention (keep in mind it's unlikely you'll affect behavior if you haven't first attracted attention and achieved retention). But they do offer three main influences on behavioral change:

Stories establish the foundation for behavior change.

There's an old saying familiar to both training and salespeople: You can lead a horse to water but you can't make him drink. However, if you don't fill the water trough and let the horse know it's there he'll never drink. As we've already discussed, stories capture your audience's attention through uncommon patterns and provide associations that help your audience retain the information.

Even though a story can't force the behavior, it can make it more inevitable by insuring the audience has received and remembered all the information necessary for the change.

Stories allow the audience to visualize the change.

When reading Tan's story, it's easy to see his folly in trying to recreate the square when the animal shapes were so much more interesting. As omnipotent readers, we see the power of creative thought Tan does not. This is a visualization of the message. Have you ever heard a sports coach tell her players to "visualize" making a play? Or perhaps a mentor has encouraged you to "visualize" achieving your goals. If you can see yourself reaching a goal, you're more likely to achieve it.

Stories work on the same principle. By seeing the impact of creative thought in Tan's Tile, it becomes more attainable for us. It's a narrative way of demonstrating return on investment (ROI). ROI figures are really a way of "visualizing" the benefits of a product or service.

Stories make the change appear more acceptable and natural to the audience.

When trying to sell a product or service, one of our first instincts is often to relate a success story. It's our way of saying: "See, so and so used this service and it worked out great for them." Testimonials are a powerful tool in both sales and training because they make the results of the behavior seem more possible. "If it worked for them; it'll probably work for me." This makes adoption of the behavior easier because it's more believable.

If you keep these benefits in mind when you develop your stories, you can design the "through line" or narrative to take advantage of them. The most obvious use of stories is to capture attention. However, it's also important to make sure your stories allow the audience to visualize your theme. The story doesn't simply convey information; it also promotes it.

As you might have already guessed, it's helpful to start a project or program design by defining the desired behavior first. You can then work backwards to determine the best way to achieve their retention and attract attention. This is actually the linear path followed by the Story Planning Worksheet.

However, it's important to keep in mind that storytelling, like all creative thought can be unpredictable. You may think of a good story long before you ever have a specific use for it. For example, I knew about the Tangram puzzle at least a year before decided to use it in this book.

Keep a journal or notebook to record creative ideas. Or just reserve a section in your day planner or PDA to capture ideas. You only have to write down enough to help you remember the whole idea. The best ideas stay with you, even if you don't record all the details.

Story Components

In order to make storytelling a more practical and consistent way to affect behavior, this technique breaks stories down into five main components: theme, audience, through line, characters, and acts and scenes. Although the theme and audience of the story should be determined first, the other elements may be pursued in any order and often benefit from parallel examination.

Like the pieces that make up the shapes in Tan's Tiles, stories have several parts that can produce many forms when assembled in different ways. Although Tan's Tile and the Tangram have seven total pieces, only five are unique: a small triangle, mid-sized triangle, parallelogram and a square. We're going to use each unique piece to represent one of the five main story components.

Theme - States the main idea of the story in one sentence and three to five goals. Setting theme is the most important step in creating a story. That's why it's represented by the square. The square piece often forms the cornerstone of Tangram creations. In the cat and fox, the square is the head of the animal. In the swan, the square is the neck. The square is also the only Tangram piece that reflects the shape of the original form. Your theme should reflect the overall purpose and concept behind your story. We'll take a closer look at theme and the Theme Planning Worksheet in Chapter 6.

Audience - Examines the demographics and psychographics of the story's target audience. Audience analysis is represented by the biggest Tangram shape, the large triangle to symbolize its importance to story formation. The demographics and psychographics of your audience shape your story. Examine your audience for background, ethnicity, age, relationships and skills (BEARS). Chapter 7 examines audience analysis in more detail and introduces the Audience Analysis Worksheet.

Through line – Describes the order and flow of the story. The through line moves the audience through the content of the story through actions, events and dialog. Through line ensures the audience reads or listens from one paragraph to the next. In Tan's Tile, dialog between Tan and the other characters moves the story. The illustrations of Tan's animal shapes also help. Through line also includes the common elements used to carry the theme throughout the story. For example, this book repeatedly refers back to Tan's Tile. "Branding" is also an example of through line.

Characters - Provide figures in the story for the audience to identify with. Chapter 2 introduced the connection between the audience and the characters in a story. The audience must either identify with, or see the folly of the characters in the story. In Tan's Tile, we see Tan's folly in his quest for the square. The idea of creative thought becomes more palatable because we're "in the know" (as opposed to Tan who is in the dark). In a role play-based story the audience can actually be the central characters in a story. We'll take a closer look at through line in Chapter 9.

Acts & Scenes - Divide the topic into manageable sections. There are obvious points of division in books and chapters, sections and paragraphs. However, information in general must be broken down into manageable bits that are independent of the usual stylistic or grammatical devices. For example, this book breaks story construction into main components presented here.

Humans typically process information in three to five "bits" and never more than seven. Examine your content to determine how many bits of information exist. Make sure you have broken down each topic into manageable sections of information that your audience can comprehend and remember. This technique is explored further in a later chapter of the book.

Diversion: Why?

Answering the "Why?" Question

Stories help to answer the age-old educational question of "why?" Ever since we were children in class we've been asking "why" in response to education and information.

> **"Why do we need to know this?"**
> **"Why do I need to buy this product?"**
> **"Why should I care about this?"**

And, of course the age-old favorite:

> **"Will this be on the test?"**

Stories provide a specific illustration that answers the "why" question. They demonstrate the topic "in action" and its results.

7 Secrets

- We can't directly affect behavior; human motivations are unpredictable.
- To change behavior, you have to define the behavior first.
- Measurable objectives (for behavioral change) contain actions, conditions and standards.
- To change behavior, we have to first attract attention and effectively deliver a message.
- Stories lay the foundation for change.
- Stories allow the audience to visualize the change.
- Stories make the target behavior more acceptable.

Exercises

Fill in the Blanks

1. Defining the affect behavior involves constructing
_____.

2. Objectives contain three main elements:

a. _____

b. _____

c. _____

3. Human motivation and behavior is
_____.

4. Stories lay the _____ for change.

5. Stories make the target behavior more
_____ to the audience.

Discussion Questions

1. Under what conditions will you probably not be able to affect behavior?

2. What are some strategies for helping the audience visualize the intended behavior?

3. In what ways can you make your target behavior seem more acceptable to your audience?

Chapter 5 – Story Types

Chapter Objectives

- Construct a type of story based on structure, purpose and style.
- Select the appropriate story based on the current situation.

Chapter Overview

This chapter provides a new way to think of story type based on the idea of practical storytelling. This method is based on the idea of classifying stories based on structure, purpose and style. The chapter builds on this foundation to link the specific aspects of story type for the current situation.

Classifying Stories

There are many different methodologies to classifying stories into type. Most derive from the specific goals of those developing the classification. For example, academic classifications often break story types down into various archetypes or classical story forms, such as the hero epic. Another variation is to classify story types according to theme, such as the classic Oedipal theme (the supplanting of a parent by their child).

While these forms are universal and intellectually stimulating, they can be impractical for everyday use. For example, it would be difficult to convince your manager to let you tell a fable at the next board meeting to explain your new inventory process.

The business world often takes a more utilitarian outlook on stories and classifies them according to use: corporate history, joke, customer experience, best practices, etc. While the goal of each of these forms is immediately apparent, these classifications can be limiting in scope.

As mentioned above, modern documentary filmmaking has managed to carve a niche telling this type of story on networks such as the History Channel and the Discovery Channel. A corporate history of Hershey or Disney on one of these channels isn't just interesting because of the products. Corporate histories tend to take on a certain, methodical format. As a result, most of them are fairly boring. The histories shown on television are interesting because of the way the story is told.

Modern documentary makers often draw from the literary story types to make a normally dry subject more interesting. Corporate histories can be examples of the classic Horatio Alger "rags-to-riches" format. This story type dates back many centuries and can be found in Greek myths and even the Bible.

Business story classifications provide a workable framework and purpose, but academic archetypes hold interest. Practical storytelling must utilize a story development format that draws from both traditions to balance originality and creativity with practicality.

The following framework breaks the concept of "story type" into three distinct areas: structure, purpose and style. Each of these can be combined in different ways to create different results.

Structure

Structure describes the physical way the story is constructed or the "through line." All stories have a beginning, middle and end, but the presentation of those components and the fluidity of their boundaries differ based on the format. Shorter stories blend all three components together, while longer stories generally have well defined sections or "acts." A story structure provides you with a general set of parameters.

Structure also taps into our shared storytelling heritage, creating an instant connection with your audience. Whether or not we consciously realize it, we all look for these three sections in every story. We feel cheated or confused when one of the sections are missing or inadequately developed.

Anecdote

Anecdotes are generally short stories in which all three components are contained within a single act.

They are generally five to fifteen minutes in length (sometimes less). The safety-themed car commercial used early in this book is an example of an anecdote. Another example would be a brief story you tell in an interview to demonstrate a job skill or strength.

Episode

Episodes are generally longer than anecdotes and contain more defined separation between the beginning, middle and end of the story. Sometimes an episode may combine beginning and middle or middle and the end. Episodes are generally twenty to thirty minutes long. The half hour television show is a classic example of an episode (hence the term "television episode"). Each of the three acts is generally separated by a commercial break.

However, the television show is actually a modernization of the written short story. Episodes often follow repeatable patterns. For example, every Sherlock Holmes story begins with Holmes and Watson in their office where they typically meet with a client. During the middle of the story they employ a number of methods to solve the crime. The end of the story is a scene in which Holmes explains exactly how and why the killer committed the crime.

Narrative

Narratives are longer, more developed stories with a clear distinction between acts. The typical narrative runs a minimum of thirty minutes and the narrative structure contains three acts. Characters and plot lines are introduced in Act I, leading up to a major plot point or twist. Following this first major plot point the characters spent the middle section of the narrative overcoming a series of challenges until a second major plot point occurs.

All plot lines are resolved in the third and final act. In traditional narratives, such as books and plays, these three acts are often evenly spaced. However, in modern storytelling, such as in movies and television, the trend is to make the second act twice as long as the first and third acts.

Purpose

Purpose refers to the goal or "point" of telling the story. The best way to discover your purpose is simply to ask: Why am I telling this story? What do I hope to accomplish? However, in most cases a story has a primary and a secondary purpose. If you approach a member of the opposite sex in a bar and tell them a humorous story about you and your friends, the primary purpose may be to entertain but the secondary purpose may be to motivate the person get to know you better.

When dealing with primary and secondary purposes, be careful to consider both when planning your story. We've all seen extremely entertaining commercial that don't motivate anyone to buy the product (or even remember the product).

Entertaining

This purpose seeks mainly to bring enjoyment to the audience. There are generally two types of entertaining stories: comedies and dramas. Most stories today blend the two. In modern storytelling, only opera and operatic stories present only comedy or only drama. There are several methods of maintaining an entertaining story such as humor, irony and suspense.

Educational

This purpose seeks to teach the audience a lesson, skill or idea. Classic educational stories have a "moral" or specific rule, often literally stated at the end of the story. Modern educational stories are more subtle and guide the audience to reach their own conclusion. In a formal training setting educational stories are usually followed by discussion questions (known as the Socratic method).

Inspirational

This purpose seeks to stir a certain feeling or reaction in the audience. Inspirational and Motivational stories are similar. However, an inspirational story doesn't necessarily have to lead to a specific course of action. Inspirational stories seek to invigorate an audience and are often the first step before a motivational story, especially in the corporate environment. For example, a program in change management often begins with a more inspirational story, before the new business model or plan is announced.

Motivational

This purpose seeks to induce the audience into performing a specific action or set of actions. All motivational stories must contain a "call to action." The call to action is a specific task given to the audience following the story. In the case of the car commercial, the call to action might be something like: "see your local Marvel Motors dealer for special incentives on the Guardian, the safest car in America."

As indicated above, any of these purposes can be combined to create a primary and secondary purpose. The most common pairing is entertaining and any of the other three purposes. However, give careful thought to which purpose should be your primary purpose. Educational, inspirational and motivational purposes almost always trump an entertaining purpose in any type of pairing. If you're trying to sell a product or win an argument, that's your primary purpose. Telling a story that is also entertaining is a means to that end.

Style

The style of a story refers to its approach. The approach should remain consistent throughout the entire structure. This makes it easier for the audience to follow. Because storytelling exists as an integral part of the human condition, we instantly recognize certain style patterns.

Almost all historical stories follow a specific pattern: they begin with a climax of events. Immediately following the opening, the clock is turned back and each event is presented in a linear mode until we reach the climax again. This time the climax is examined more thoroughly, followed by the aftermath.

All journalistic stories begin with a lead: dog bites man (or man bites dog), followed by deeper and deeper levels of detail about the story based on who, what, when where and why.

Mythical stories tend to involve a central character that overcomes long odds to achieve greatness. Along the way they face a series of trials and experience a short periods of success followed by an even larger trial. Finally after learning many lessons along the way they triumph.

At first this continual re-use of the same patterns can seem constraining. For example, why can't we tell a historical story completely in reverse? Actually these shared and repeated patterns are liberating. They free us up from the time it would normally take to set up the style of the story itself.

If we told a historical story in complete reverse, it would take the audience awhile to understand the pattern of the story. During this time they would be concentrating on understanding the style of the story, rather than the substance of the story.

This is not to say you can't experiment. Just be sure your goal, audience and environment provide room for experimentation. Creative outlets such as movies, television and books tend to have a higher tolerance for experimentation.

The business world tends to prefer tried and true methods of storytelling. (It could also be argued since the movie, television and publishing industries have become big business, they too now have a lower tolerance for experimentation.)

Historical

Historical stories present a series of events in a linear fashion. "First we did this, then we did that, and it all led to the following result." Historical stories tend to dramatize facts and may even imagine conversations and events that may or may not have taken place. However, any embellishments are plausible and grounded in the events or facts serving as the basis for the story.

Historical is the most common story style because it is both accessible and flexible. The historical style draws from facts or events but adapts them to serve its own purpose. Another common trait of historical stories is the emphasis of certain aspects of the story over certain other aspects.

This emphasis tends to derive from the purpose of the story (an entertaining story may play up the more humorous parts of the story) and the storyteller (certain storytellers are people driven, others are more plot driven).

Journalistic

Journalistic is the most straightforward and utilitarian of all the story styles, although it is not linear. As mentioned above, journalistic stories always begin by stating their most important point: "customer service is the key to repeat business" or "we saved the Johnson account yesterday through some quick thinking and aggressive pricing." The point is followed by a logical sequence that provides an ever-increasing level of details.

Newspaper stories are designed so that you can decide how much detail you'd like to hear about a story. Each paragraph contains deeper and deeper details about the subject. You don't need to read the whole article to understand the main point of the story, though. An advantage of the journalistic style is that it is very scalable. A journalistic narrative can usually be scaled back to an episode or anecdote simply by removing levels of details.

Mythical

It's common for historical and journalistic stories to become mythical over time. Some people would argue all fishing stories become mythical as soon as the fishermen leave the dock. In business, the story of a company's founding often grows from historical to mythical, as do stories about the company's founder.

Most people would say Henry Ford invented the assembly line. In reality he observed an assembly line at a Chicago meat packing plant and adapted the concept to automobiles. Mythical stories are generally not as deeply bound by facts and reality as historical and journalistic stories. They are meant to convey a general idea or truth rather than a specific point (i.e. Henry Ford was innovative man who revolutionized automobile production).

Bear in mind that no matter how we classify a story, it always must contain a common set of components and characteristics to be successful. From an organizational standpoint, every story must have a beginning, middle and end (no matter how short). It must also contain key elements contained in the rest of this book.

Choosing a Story Type

Choosing the right structure, purpose and style for your story depends on three factors: the goal, the audience and the situation. At first glance this can seem like a daunting task that involves simultaneously evaluating a number of different factors. Matching the right type of story to the specific theme, audience and situation can be a challenge.

However picking the right structure, purpose and style is usually a matter of common sense. Telling your wife a mythical narrative about the record-setting northern pike your neighbor caught is probably not going to motivate her to let you buy that new bass boat. But telling her an inspirational anecdote about how the boat brought your neighbor closer to his son or daughter might be a step in the right direction.

Much of the time the path to the right story type naturally presents itself. For example, if your audience has a short attention span you can eliminate the narrative structure and perhaps even the episode structure immediately. If you're addressing a group of scientists, a mythical story may not be the best choice. If your goal is to sell a product, your purpose is always motivation (although you may choose one of the other purposes as secondary).

Knowing the strengths and weaknesses of your own storytelling ability can also help you narrow your choice of structure, purpose and style. Practice each story type in front of others (or record yourself) to determine the story types best suited to your storytelling abilities or personality. This is not to say you shouldn't try to get better at other styles.

If you're unsure of the correct combination of structure, style and purpose, try out two to three different combinations of structure, purpose and style on a test audience. Start with shorter structures and move on to longer ones. The more research and planning you do upfront, the more likely you are to come up with the right combination sooner.

Each of the three aspects mentioned above: theme, audience and environment are described at greater detail in later chapters. In the meantime, use the table below as a general guide for matching structure, purpose and style to specific situations. If your situation isn't listed, choose a similar situation.

Situation	Structure	Purpose	Style
Social intro-duction	Anecdote	Entertaining	Historical
Business intro-duction	Anecdote Episode (formal)	Educational Motivational (second meeting, learn more)	Historical Journalistic
Product pitch	Episode Narrative	Motivational /Educational	Historical Journalistic
Political debate	Anecdote	Inspirational /Educational Motivatioanl /Educational	Journalistic Mythical
First date	Anecdote	Entertaining/ Educational Entertaining/ Motivational (second date)	Historical
Sales call	Anecdote Episode	Educational Motivational	Journalistic
TV or Radio Ad	Anecdote	Motivational /Educational Motivational /Entertaining	Journalistic
Business speech	Anecdote Episode	Motivational /Educational Inspirational /Educational Motivational /Entertaining Inspirational	Historical Mythical

		/ Entertaining	
Training Program	Anecdote Episode Narrative	Educational/ Entertaining Educational/ Motivational	Historical Journalistic

Diversion: Return of the One-hour Drama

People are always coming up with new twists on structure and style. When Dick Wolfe created the original *Law and Order* series, he wanted to do an hour drama but was worried about the attention span of the audience. At the time, hour-long dramas had largely faded from the television schedule in favor of half hour comedies. The answer for Wolfe was to create an hour-long drama that essentially consisted of two separate half hour shows.

The first half hour of the show opens with the discovery of a body, followed by a police investigation. At the end of the half hour the police arrest the suspect. The second half hour of the show typically opens in the district attorney's office and follows the DA and his assistant's efforts to actually convict the suspect.

The end of the second half hour either coincides with the verdict or a short commentary on the verdict. This clever way to revive the one-hour drama is now one of the longest running television shows and subsequently re-opened the door for one hour dramas throughout the prime time schedule.

7 Secrets

- Most story type methodologies are based around the goal of those who created them.
- Stories can be interesting when the right type of story is used for the situation.
- Story type is derived from three parameters: structure, purpose and style.
- The three types of structure are anecdote, episode and purpose.
- The four types of purpose are entertaining, educational, inspirational and motivational.
- The three types of style are historical, journalistic and mythical.
- Always match your structure, purpose and style to the specific situation.

Exercises

Fill in the Blanks

1. The three main story structures are:

a. _____

b. _____

c. _____

2. The most commonly used story purpose is _____.

3. The style of the story refers to its _____.

4. The three main story styles are:

a. _____

b. _____

c. _____

5. The right story type is composed of three elements: _____, _____ and _____.

Discussion Questions

1. How is the mythical story style used within modern contexts? How is it similar to traditional myths such as the Odyssey? How is it different?

2. What is the best way to balance purpose, structure and style within a story type? Are any of these elements incompatible with each other? Why or why not?

Part 2 – Story Construction

Chapter 6: Develop a Theme

Chapter Objectives:

- Describe the importance of theme as the foundation for story formation.
- Use the Story Planning Worksheet and the Theme Planning Worksheet to develop a story theme.

Chapter Overview:

This chapter examines story theme and theme construction in more detail. It explains how to develop a one-sentence theme for your story using the Story Planning Worksheet, Theme Planning Worksheet and Brainstorming Guide.

The Importance of Theme

We've already discussed the importance of theme. In this chapter we're going to take a closer look at theme creation. The key to good storytelling is the development of a clear and concise theme. Theme transforms your story from simply entertaining to deeply meaningful. Ideally, you should be able to state your theme in one sentence or less.

Don't confuse theme with synopsis or summary. It's helpful to complete a one-paragraph synopsis of the story and its goals, or a one-page summary for a longer story. However, you should be able to state the core concept behind the story as well as the overall goal in just a few words. To construct a theme you need two core components:

- The goal of the project or program (the affect behavior or objective).
- The main idea for the story (narrative or metaphor).

Whether the main idea for the story comes directly from your mind (or the mind of your team) or from a file or notebook of your ideas, it should be linked to the objective. Chapter 3 covers the specific steps in creating an objective: actions, conditions and standards. In this chapter we're going to pick up from there and discuss how to derive the rest of the story idea using three worksheets:

- The Story Planning Worksheet
- The Theme Planning Worksheet
- The Brainstorming Guide

All of the worksheets mentioned in this book are available in Appendix D or as full size (8.5x11) downloadable PDF documents at the website www.practicalstorytelling.com.

Story Planning

Story planning begins by stating the goal or objective of the story. This objective is the primary purpose of the story. Although there are secondary purposes related to attention and retention, the sum total of the story should be focused on the specific goal. This usually derives from the affect behavior.

For example in the museum illustration presented later I this book, the main goal of the story within the brochure is to make the audience interested enough to contact the museum or more receptive when a member of the museum contacts them. It's not to directly get people to sign up for the program. That's a subtle but important distinction affecting the way content is created, organized and presented.

If we don't keep the main goal in mind, the result is that distracting elements appear in the story. The goal in Tan's Tile is to demonstrate the power of creative thought; all the elements in the story relate to that end. Tan never experiences a moment of "enlightenment," because we don't need to actually see that for the story to be affective. In fact, the story is stronger because Tan doesn't experience this realization. The audience is in a position of superior knowledge over Tan because we see the value in creatively arranging the tiles. This motivates the audience to identify with the theme of the story: creative thought.

Similarly, the museum brochure does not discuss any details about the typical cost of setting up a display. It doesn't have to since its purpose isn't to close the deal. It's just to introduce the idea. The person following-up can discuss pricing. By contrast, a point of purchase website must provide pricing because the entire transaction most likely takes place within a single session.

Use the Story Planning Worksheet to record your objective(s) and begin the creative process of story development. Section SI of the worksheet provides spaces for up to three objectives. More objectives than that are difficult to combine into one central theme. If you really have more than three main objectives, you may want to split a single program into multiple ones.

Also keep in mind the scale with which you're working. Start at the highest layer and work your way down. If you're developing a training manual, begin at the overall theme for the program. Then develop a theme for each chapter or module. If the modules are large, you may have to develop themes for subsections within the modules.

In section SII of the worksheet, begin to think of any examples and/or metaphors to demonstrate the major points of the objective. (Hint: It's usually easier to come up with specific answers.) Don't worry about organization at this point; just get your ideas on paper. The next worksheet helps you pull a theme from these notes. Use the right side of the worksheet for brainstorming.

Review the ideas you've recorded in section SII and record specific ideas to attract attention in section SIII. Look at your ideas in the previous section and expand them. As you expand single ideas, you'll be able to start weaving them together and form the basis for a longer story.

Building Theme

Use the Theme Planning Worksheet to begin organizing your raw ideas from the previous worksheet. By the end of the Theme Planning Worksheet you should have a one-sentence statement of your theme. You'll begin by copying your objectives(s) into section TI of this worksheet. Remember you're going to combine (if necessary) and couple these objectives with the story idea after you develop it.

Circle the best ideas and metaphors from sections SII and SIII on the Story Planning Worksheet and copy them to section TII of the Theme Planning Worksheet. Experiment with these ideas until you have one or two that can carry the entire objective. Perhaps you have one idea that can serve as a "parent" for the other ideas. Or you may invent a new idea that summarizes several of the existing ones.

Use the Brainstorming Guide to assist you in these activities. This worksheet presents six main ways to think about your ideas. One or a combination of these techniques should help you start to flesh out your ideas for the story. Another technique is to work with other people. You can either fill in the worksheet as a group, or fill in preliminary thoughts and then ask a colleague to reply.

Let's take a closer look at each of the six brainstorming methods included on the guide (For examples of these methods, see the Brainstorming Guide.):

Outline Method

One of the most traditional brainstorming methods, outlining involves recording the largest ideas behind a project and then breaking them down into smaller items underneath. You can use bullets or numbering. If you have difficulty starting, use the objectives as the main bullets. Add sub-bullets to flesh out the core ideas.

Write more specific illustrations of each as sub-bullets. Continue drilling down as far as you can. Add new main bullets as necessary. The outline method also works well with any of the other methods. You can use outlines to organization and clarify ideas.

Free-write Method

Free-writing is exactly what it sounds like: you pick up a pen and just start writing about the topic. Go as long as you can without stopping. Don't pause to correct or reread what you've written. When you can't write anymore, put down the pen and take a rest.

After taking time to reflect, read back over your writing and circle any keywords or phrases. You may also want to highlight useful parts. You can use one of the other methods to further organize your writing.

Research Method

The research method is self-explanatory. Begin with the objectives or main ideas of your story and research them. You can use the library or Internet for your search. Record any facts or ideas you find, along with their sources. Use one of the other methods to further organize your work. To begin your search, circle the keywords within your objectives or goals.

Search on these words first and then search for synonyms of these words. If you're using the Internet, it may help to include words such as "article" or "journal" in some of the searches. This is more likely to return journal or periodicals as opposed to random links. Hopefully you'll identify two to three main resources. Use these main resources to search for additional information by circling more keywords within them.

Circle Diagram Method

In this method you record main and "satellites" ideas within circles. The circles are then connected with lines to show relationships. Begin by drawing several large circles. Write one of the main ideas or objectives within each circle. Around each circle, write derivative ideas based on the idea in the circle.

Circle these ideas and then write as many derivative ideas as you can. You can use circle size to denote the relative importance of each idea. When you're finished or as you go along, draw lines from circle to circle to indicate any connections. You can also clarify connections by writing on the connecting lines.

Word Association Method

This is a simple method, but may be able to get you started if you're having trouble. From the main ideas or objectives, choose three keywords and write them down. Read each word and write as many other words as you can think of next to it.

When you stall out, go onto the next word. When you've worked through all the words, start circling the best of the related words and perform word association on them. Continue until you are able to start organizing the words using one of the other methods.

Organizational Chart Method

Organizational charts are similar to outlining but are more visual. Begin by placing your main ideas or objectives in the top boxes. Place subtopics in smaller boxes underneath and connected by lines. Continue to work your way down as far as you can go.

All of the methods above are presented and explained on the Braining Storming Guide included in this book. Gradually refine your theme using the methods presented above until you are able to create one sentence that pairs an overall story idea or example with the single, overall objective.

When you are ready to do so, fill this one sentence theme into section TIII of the Theme Planning Workshop. Add any keywords that go with the theme for future reference.

Diversion: Sources of Inspiration

You can get plenty of story inspiration from books, movies and television. These media types represent common literary traditions we all share. Playing off a popular show or movie provides instant recognition among your audience and is almost like having an inside joke that everyone gets.

Also, many of these programs are the retelling of older stories to which we can always relate. If you're having trouble thinking of ideas, you may want to take a break and go to the movies. Remember, they need to attract attention too.

7 Secrets

- State the theme of your story in one sentence or less.
- The theme directs development of the story as a whole.
- The theme combines the main goals or objectives of the story with a central design idea.
- Central design ideas can come from metaphors and examples drawn from the information content.
- Develop central design ideas by brainstorming.
- There are six main brainstorming methods: Outline, Circle Diagram, Free-write, Word Association, Research and Organizational Chart.
- Use the Theme Planning Worksheet, Story Planning Worksheet and the Brainstorming Guide to develop a theme.

Exercises

Fill in the Blanks

1. _____ directs the development of the story as a whole.

2. The theme combines the _____ and _____ _____.

3. The central design idea can often be developed through _____.

4. Three methods of brainstorming are:

a. _____

b. _____

c. _____

Discussion Questions

1. State the theme of your six favorite books, movies or television shows in one sentence or less.

2. Are there any central design ideas in your employee handbook that could be used to make it more interesting?

3. How can the six brainstorming methods presented in this chapter be combined for more effective results?

Chapter 7: Analyze the Audience

Chapter Objectives:

- Describe the importance and impact of audience analysis.
- List and define the five points in BEARS audience analysis.
- Use the Audience Analysis Worksheet as a starting point for audience analysis.
- Choose a story type based on the results of audience analysis.

Chapter Overview:

This chapter examines the specific areas of audience analysis using the BEARS method. It introduces the BEARS Audience Analysis Worksheet and discusses how to choose a story type based on the target audience.

Different Perspectives

Each member of Tan's family sees a different animal in the shapes. This is partly due to the arrangement of the tiles, but also because of a person's unique perspective.

For example, Tan's son interprets his shape as a fox, while Tan's daughter believes hers to be a cat. However, these shapes are very similar. Tan's son relates the shape to the fox he saw in the garden. Perhaps Tan's daughter has a kitten of her own. Even the swan Tan's wife sees could be a goose or another type of waterfowl. Each audience sees a distinct shape in the tile pieces.

Just as Tan's family interprets the shapes in different ways, audiences interpret stories in different ways. Storytelling is most effective when you choose the best story and story type for the specific audience.

In order to choose the story type and "flavor" the story, you must first analyze your audience. When analyzing your audience, consider the following factors:

(B)ackground - Give some general thought to who these people are. People you work with? A specific trade group? Where are they from? How do they feel about the current setting?

(E)thnicity - This area is important for two main reasons: 1) Language-related errors, such as difficulties because of accent, vocabulary or expressions. 2) Culture-related errors, such as the varying relationships between teacher and student.

(A)ge - Think not only about the ages within the audience, but the relationship between their age and your age. What generations are attending your speech? What are the common values of that generation(s)?

(R)elationships - What is the relationship between members of the audience? What hierarchies exist within it? What is your relationship to the audience? Are you a vender? A client? Are you speaking to people in a greater position of power? A lesser position of power?

(S)kills - Consider this in conjunction with your topic. How much do they know about the topic already? What new information do you have to offer?

Together, these elements make up the acronym BEARS. The BEARS acronym is an example of getting into long-term memory using association. If you remember the word BEARS, you'll most likely remember the areas each letter stand for.

Determining these factors is a matter of asking the right question sets. Included with the Audience Analysis Worksheet is a set of questions for each of the areas above. You don't necessarily have to answer every question for each area but they are a good starting point.

A full list of questions for each of these areas is available in Appendix D, as part of the Audience Analysis Worksheet.

Learning About Your Audience

There are four main ways to learn more about your audience: research, interviews, surveys and a welcome activity (for individual groups). No matter which method or methods you choose, always begin with some degree of research to lay a foundation.

Research

Usually the least expensive method of learning about your audience is research, particularly research on the Internet. Begin with basic facts such as age, position, trade and geographic location. Research each of these areas independently. You can start with a simple Internet keyword search using an engine like Google (www.google.com).

In the search results, look specifically for academic and trade journal articles. You may even want to include the word "paper," "journal" or "article" in your search to filter out some of the clutter. Once you've researched each area, begin to synthesize the areas together into a more complete picture using the Outline Method, Circle Diagram or Organizational Diagram Method (presented in Chapter 6.)

Interviews

The best way to get to know people is to talk with them. If it's a large audience, try to interview at least a sampling. Often you can do this through personal contacts or networking. Do you have a friend who is in your target audience? Or perhaps you have a friend or a friend of a friend in the target audience.

Another technique is to contact specific people in the target audience and request an informational interview. Specifically you're not trying to sell anything; you'd just like to know more about their business and the problems they face. You can actually make this an even exchange by offering them information in return. If you're building a training program, interview participants get a preview of the material.

If you're building a marketing or sales campaign you can offer a free informal strategy session with the interviewee. You can also offer a premium or gift. This is particularly effective in a consulting environment.

Always be completely prepared when conducting an interview and have your questions written out beforehand. This ensures you'll get all the answers you need and is courteous towards the interviewee.

Surveys

A more formal way of gathering information about your audience is to conduct a survey. This is often the hardest and most costly method. However, it can yield the best results, especially if you survey a large sample of your audience. (The other good thing about surveys is that the survey itself raises awareness about you and your product or service.)

Follow these guidelines when developing a survey:

- Keep the survey to one page.
- Convey only one thought per question.
- Try to offer some incentive for filling out the survey.
- Plan your sample size based on getting only a 15% response.

Welcome Activity

Sometimes called an "icebreaker," this technique is a solution when you've had no time to analyze your audience beforehand. Icebreakers can warm up an audience and put them more at ease. They also allow for a transition time between normal, daily activities and the purpose of the group.

Icebreakers are metaphorical activities designed to get participants thinking and talking. Within these activities, audience members will often reveal information about themselves, particularly in smaller groups. You can also use welcome activities during surveys and focus groups. One of the best things about welcome activities or icebreakers is that hundreds have already been developed. They're also easy to modify and tailor to your specific purpose.

Whichever method you choose, audience analysis really comes down to asking the right questions. Use the questions with the BEARS Audience Analysis Worksheet to direct your activities. You don't have to answer every question for every project, but you should initially consider each question. Make a conscious decision and have justification for including or excluding a question.

Addressing Your Audience

Not every story begins "once upon a time" or features an animated character. The first question is "what's the story?" The second is "what type of story is appropriate?" Since the audience for this book is varied, it requires a story that potentially appeals to a wide range of people.

The audience includes training, sales and marketing people, so a specific industry example or story would have isolated at least one portion of the audience. Specifically, choose the story type on three factors:

- The audience.
- The program goal.
- The personality or branding of your organization.

Sustaining more than one story or example is difficult. In a book with a wide target like this one, you must either develop a story with wide appeal or split the longer story into several targeted anecdotes. Tan's Tile has a wider appeal. It purposely uses the style of a fable or parable, because this type of story is common in the literary traditions of all peoples. Even though the legend of Tangram is Chinese, most other cultures recognize the genre itself and can identify with it.

However, this is not to say that all your stories should be universal or generic. While it's appealing to avoid excluding anyone, it's not always the smartest decision. If your audience analysis does identify a specific target for a program, develop the story to speak directly to that target. If you need to deliver the program to a different group, you can always salvage the informational portions of the content and weave them into a different story.

That's why this book tries to provide several examples for each point. However, if research showed most readers share certain characteristics, it may be worthwhile to retool the book to appeal specifically to those chracteristics. If it sounds like you're going to be a slave to the demographics, in a sense you're right.

Delivering an appropriate story to your audience is crucial. Although most audiences welcome humor in a presentation, some do not. For example, when marketing a mini-van, humor is almost expected. However, you probably wouldn't use humor to market a high-end luxury car. Most training programs on sexual harassment include little or no humor because of the seriousness of the topic.

These are not necessarily hard and fast rules, of course. Lexus used humor in a past campaign emphasizing the safety of their cars. The ad focused on the "other drivers" out there. It was a smart campaign because we wanted to identify with the "more skilled" Lexus drivers. Even in this case though, the story and humor were constructed carefully to elicit a specific affect on the audience.

The story type is also chosen based on the goal of the program. Using stories requires creative thought. Therefore, the story of Tan's Tile used in this book emphasizes creative thought. Just like the Lexus commercial, it's designed so that we want to identify with the more creative members of Tan's family, rather than Tan himself who only wants to re-create his original square. The fable or parable story type works well for this type of chapter.

Finally, the story should reflect the personality of your organization. If you have an organization rich in tradition, use that tradition when delivering your messages. Draw on stories from your past to emphasize ideas for the present and future. If you have a reputation for safety and stability, use those themes in your story. Each story should also contribute to the overall brand strategy of your organization.

Branding is important in both training and sales. I'm sure the sales folks are shaking their heads right now. The training folks may be cocking their heads to one side and wondering. But branding is important in training too. Your reputation and the reputation of your company or department precede you into the classroom (real or virtual).

There is one exception to branding: sometimes organizations use creative thought and stories to "break out" or remove existing perceptions of the organization. A story that contrasts your company's usual message or personality can re-invigorate the audience. However, check your audience's receptiveness to such a change before using it. You can do this using the audience analysis methods presented above.

Choosing a Story Type

Choose a story type that best fits your audience, goals and organizational personality. Stories range along three main dimensions: formality, length and complexity. The topic provides several clues and correlations to determine these dimensions.

Formality is derived from the topic and audience. Topics such as "Effective Presentations" and "Effective Writing" can be told in less formal stories, such as the comic strip characters used in the sample program. Other subjects like a medical system or company history require a more formal approach.

We must also account for the tolerance of the audience. Certain groups may be unreceptive of a less formal story. A scenario-based program is an example of a more formal storytelling technique. In a scenario the participant is given a role within a reality-based story. Role-playing is a similar technique.

The amount of material determines length. The simplest of the three dimensions, length is determined by dividing and sub-dividing a program into groups of three to five complete bits of information, each definable in an action-oriented objective. However not all story types are sustainable over certain lengths. Stories perform most effectively and efficiently when used consistently.

Complexity is the most difficult dimension to calculate and deal with, especially in longer stories. More complex topics generally require more complex stories. The story in a complex program anchors the material in metaphor and example. This helps the user visualize the material.

Creativity is an abstract topic. Sometimes a simple story can best demonstrate a difficult topic. Such is the case in Tan's Tile. It's a simple story, but it illustrates creativity. Once you begin to read the book material, it's also clear the story has more levels than it appears.

The other method of handling complex stories is to rely on real life examples. We teach children to tie shoes by showing them how to tie the knot step by step. This technique scales well to larger tasks. This is sometimes referred to as "progressive" learning. You demonstrate one step, followed by that step with the next one.

This technique works for longer-term sales and marketing messages as well. Your first message captures the audience attention. Each subsequent message reviews the previous one and presents the next point. This is why advertisers often use a series of commercials built around the one central theme.

In other cases the story is a simple one. A series of concise and practical job aids may be the whole narrative. In this case the audience themselves are the main characters and the plot is the job to be completed.

Animated characters or comics don't help in this case. However locating the task-based "through line" of how to complete the job does. Just as a story must resolve itself, the learner must complete a specific sequence of events to resolve the task at hand.

The Story Type Worksheet helps you analyze your story based on formality, length and complexity. You can derive the formality rating directly from audience analysis. The other two dimensions are plotted from the material itself.

Using Multiple Stories

A previous chapter compared stories to sandpaper. Stories can breakdown a topic the same way a sheet of sandpaper wears down the outer layers of a piece of wood. Just as harder and thicker woods require higher-grade sandpaper, more complex topics require more intricate stories.

However, if you don't have the right grade of sandpaper you can still use multiple sheets of a lesser grade. It just takes longer to sand down the wood. Stories work in a similar way. You can breakdown a complex topic by using a series of smaller stories and examples.

In fact, many complicated sanding jobs require multiple grades of sandpaper to get a finer, smoother result. You start with a high-grade sandpaper to take out the major bumps and dents and then switch to a finer grain to finish the wood.

In most cases you'll use multiple stories, examples and metaphors to breakdown a topic.

This book uses Tan's Tile as a central story and theme but includes a number of support examples and metaphors throughout the book. The sandpaper metaphor we've been discussing and the cat example in Chapter 2 support the main story. In addition, there are dozens of small, individual examples used to illustrate specific points.

After you have rated your topic using the Story Type Worksheet, rate the individual stories or major examples you plan to use. The total complexity rating of each story, example and metaphor you plan to use should at least equal the complexity level of the story. For safety's sake, it's good to make the story total ten to twenty-five percent   higher   than   the   topic   total.

Diversion: How Do You Know If You've Got It Right?

The best way to know if you're choosing the right story is to pilot a preliminary version among members or a sampling of your audience. This can be a formal test of a prototype of the project or program, or just a "sanity-check" in which you ask a perspective participant: "What do you think of this?" or "Does this make sense?"

Stories work best when they are developed iteratively, that is, in small sections containing parallel activities. Once you've developed your theme, run it by some colleagues and audience members. After you have an idea for the through line, develop a small section and deliver it to a small group. Make any necessary modifications.

It also helps to address the high-risk items first. For example, if you're planning to use animated characters test out a short version first to make sure the audience would accept this type of style.

7 Secrets

- Analyze your audience for background, ethnicity, age, relationships and skills.
- Use the Audience Analysis Worksheet and Audience Question Guide to examine your target audience.
- Choose your story type based on the target audience, program goal and organizational personality or brand.
- Stories range along three main dimensions: formality, length and complexity.
- Formality relates directly to the target audience.
- The story's complexity level derives from the complexity of the topic.
- You can use multiple stories to deliver more complex messages.

Exercises

Fill in the Blanks

1. Choose your story type based on the _____
_____.

2. Audience analysis includes the following measurements:

a. _____

b. _____

c. _____

d. _____

e. _____

3. Four methods of audience analysis are:

a. _____

b. _____

c. _____

d. _____

4. All audience analysis should begin with _____.

5. Stories can be analyzed along three dimensions:

a. _____

b. _____

c. _____

Discussion Questions

1. What do you know about the audience for your current training, sales or marketing program?

2. What audience analysis methods work best for your target audience(s) and why?

3. What types of stories would be most acceptable to your   audience?

Chapter 8 – Design the Characters

Chapter Objectives

- Construct characters that are identifiable, involving and experience growth.
- Locate and modify characters from other sources.

Chapter Overview

This chapter introduces the three key elements of good characters: identifiable, involving and experience growth. It specifically provides a series of ten questions to help you develop your own characters. Each of these questions is answered using the example story, Tan's Tile.

About Characters

Compelling characters are an important element in any story. When telling a story from our own experience we are the central character. There is instant appeal anytime the storyteller (or narrator) is the central character. This is why stories from our own lives are often the easiest and most successful to tell.

This is also the reason why many storytellers make themselves the main character even in stories that didn't originally happen to them. There's something naturally intriguing about a person telling his or her own story. If the people around you didn't find you compelling, they probably wouldn't be talking to you in the first place.

A common character mistake is relying too heavily on plot. Many storytellers assume the action or events within a story can inherently make a character involving. A story with an interesting plot can keep the audience engaged and entertained but it is unlikely to educate or motivate. In these cases the plot actually overpowers the characters, causing us to focus too much on the activity within the story and not the point of the story.

Compelling Characters

Making the other characters in the story compelling can be more of a challenge. The longer and more involved the story, the more you have to concentrate on creating good characters. Compelling characters have the following characteristics: they are identifiable, involving and experience growth.

Identifiable

Have you ever watched a movie and continually kept mixing up two of the characters? This often happens if the characters are secondary and played by similar actors. This is a case of unidentifiable characters and it often happens when writers and directors "fill out" their stories with one-dimensional and stereotypical figures. Any character that has dialog or a key action within your story must be identifiable. There must be some recognizable trait or quality for the audience to associate with that character.

The "catch phrase" is a shallow but tried and true method of providing a character with a recognizable trait. There is often something visual like a piece of clothing such as Columbo's raincoat or Indiana Jones' Fedora. On a more subtle level, characters can be identifiable based on the way they speak or act. For example, a character may repeatedly approach problems slowly and deliberately. After the first couple of times we recognize that quality in the character.

One of the easiest ways to create identifiable characters is to use the fundamental principles discussed in the first chapter. Remember that going outside of normal patterns makes someone instantly more recognizable on a base cognitive level. In addition to his raincoat, Columbo is instantly recognizable because of the methodical way he examines a crime scene and the way he is able to pick out details many people would miss. (Here we see yet another take on the "whodunit" format.)

Involving

Your characters do not have to be likeable but they do have to be interesting. Actually, we often find characters we hate more involving than characters we like. The concept of involving characters is sometimes confused with recognizable characters. A character can be memorable but not be involving.

Columbo is involving because he uses an uncommon and slower paced method to capture a murderer. He often plays the fool to leave the suspect with a feeling of false security. He's also a devoted husband and an all around nice guy. We want him to catch the bad guy (and not just because the bad guy has murdered someone).

This is an example of positive involvement and the opposite of the case of Tan's Tile. In Tan's Tile we are involved with the character of Tan as we wait for him to discover the folly of his ways. This is an example of negative involvement. We are positively involved with Columbo because we like who he is and what he is doing. We are negatively involved with Tan because we'd rather see him change and do something else.

Growth

In most cases, at least the main character in any story must grow in some way. This is true for even the shortest anecdote. Growth usually occurs when the main character surmounts some type of challenge, overcomes a problem, or learns an important lesson. Often they must go against their own nature to achieve these ends.

Growth is a natural theme in all of our lives. We physical grow up and age throughout life. We also grow mentally as we learn new things and realize new achievements. These are the so-called "rights of passage" such as graduating from school, getting a job, raising a family, buying a home, advancing in our career,, etc.

Within each of these larger goals are several smaller ones. For example, raising a family entails a steady series of challenges and learning experiences such as birth, adolescence and graduation. The milestones of our children are especially powerful because they echo our own experiences.

Similarly, we look for growth within the characters in a story. Without growth, we may find the story entertaining (especially if it contains elements we like such as romance, action, etc.) but not completely fulfilling. Educational and motivational stories almost never work if the characters within them do not grow in some way. It is this growth that delivers the final message of the theme.

Character Construction

There are a number of specific steps you can take to create strong characters. Naturally, these steps should be scaled based on the structure of your story. The characters in an anecdote are certainly not as developed as those in a narrative.

However, if you use the same characters repeatedly in several anecdotes or episodes it's worthwhile to invest more time into developing them. This is a common technique used by professional storytellers and writers. They develop a core set of strong characters and then re-use those characters throughout all of their tales.

Use the following steps to create compelling characters (each includes an example of how the question was answered for Tan's Tile):

1. Invent a character backstory.

The more you know about what happens in a characters life, the more complete they'll appear within a story. This includes events that occur before and after the timeframe of the story. It's also easier to write dialog and exactly how a character would react in a situation. Start with a simple timeline of the character's life with key events. Some of these may be standard, others specific to the character. The more events you describe the more you'll learn about your character.

From Tan's Tile - Tan is the emperor of China during an early dynasty, with an empire comprising only a few provinces. He inherited this post from his father. Maintaining peace and improving infrastructure are the main goals of his administration. He keeps a low public profile and relies heavily on his appointed officials and bureaucrats to maintain order and carry out his instructions. This allows him ample time to concentrate on raising his own family and maintaining the gardens around the palace. Both of these areas give Tan great pride.

2. Determine the core values.

Characters have a set of core values - just like real people. Usually a few key values can provide guidance for how the character as a whole would react or speak in a given situation. For example, does the character place more value on career or on family? Given the choice, would they risk their own life to save another?

On a more practical level, how do they handle everyday situations? Is the character more of a leader or a more of a manager? Given the choice, would they hire someone who was a good salesman but knew nothing about the product or someone who knew everything about the product but with no sales experience?

From Tan's Tile - Tan's core values include the importance of family and the need for discipline and order. These values are sometimes in conflict as he attempts to maintain order within his realm and gardens while also spending time with his family. He also believes in maintaining order within his family. This is sometimes a source of tension within the family and Tan often feels as though he spends much of his time playing disciplinarian rather than the doting father role.

3. Describe a pivotal moment.

Examine your character's backstory and determine what events in their personal timeline were pivotal moments for them. Did they face the death of a parent at an early age? Were they teased in school? Have they published a book? Broken a record? How did they react to these moments?

Knowing their reaction to these key moments can help you fashion their responses to the less important moments. For example, a character that repeatedly set sports records in high school may approach challenges at work more willingly than someone who spent most of their time reading books. Conversely, the bookish character may be better equipped to analyze a complex situation.

From Tan's Tile - Tan's father was killed in battle while Tan was still a young man. This moment was the culmination of the many years his father spent fighting to increase the size of his realm. During these times Tan saw very little of his father. As he grew old enough to take a role within the government, Tan thought this would be his opportunity to spend more time with his father.

However, just as Tan was assuming a post at his father's side the older man died fighting to gain control over a village in the outer lying territories. The following day Tan was crowned emperor of his father's kingdom.

4. Compare/contrast to yourself.

Another good way to flesh out a character is by comparing and contrasting the character to yourself. This provides a clear point of reference. In areas where you and the character are similar, simply have the character react or speak as you would. In areas where you and the character are different, choose an option you wouldn't normally pick.

From Tan's Tile - As emperor, Tan faces challenges I most likely will never have to face. He is much more concerned with order than I am. I also do not have a family of my own, so it can be difficult for me to fully identify with his dedication to family. I also do not place as much value on maintaining an intricate garden like Tan. However, I do share Tan's dedication when trying to complete a task. We both do not like to give up.

5. Review relationships.

Consider the character's relationships with other characters. Not only does this give you insight into the character his or herself, it also provides insight into their replies and reactions. Does this character like the other characters? Does this character respect the other characters?

For a more complex story, consider mapping out the relationships on a piece of paper or the computer. Draw circles to represent the characters and connect them with lines to represent relationships. Write the nature of the relationship on the line.

From Tan's Tile - Tan is the father of two children and husband to his wife. He is the head of his household and his empire. As such, Tan is in a position of authority over all the other characters in the story. He has the respect of all of the other characters under him.

6. List special skills.

Everybody has talents and skills. Listing these qualities beforehand is always easier than making them up as you go along. The danger in not already knowing what your characters can and can't reasonably do is that you may be tempted to give your characters new skills at opportune times to work yourself out of a jam.

Imagine two characters are locked in a jail and all of a sudden one character announces he can pick locks. If the storyteller hasn't indicated this skill beforehand it looks contrived or a "cheat." Always know the skills of each character beforehand and introduce these skills subtly throughout the story – preferably before they become essential.

From Tan's Tile - Tan has strong administrative skills and is well equipped to maintain peace and order. This manifests itself both within the leadership he provides and his physical gardens.

7. List weaknesses.

Just as you listed the character's strengths, you should also list his or her weaknesses. One benefit of listing weaknesses is that it provides you with an automatic source of character growth. It can also provide you with tension points within the story, as the character must deal with a situation in which they do not have the proper skills. It also forces that character to cooperate with other characters.

From Tan's Tile - Tan's loss of his father causes him to often be too cautious and rely too heavily on the overall order of things. He rarely takes chances and sticks to "tried and true" methods.

8. Describe potential improvement.

Answer the following questions: If the character could change one thing about himself or herself, what would it be? If the character's best friend or immediate family member could change one thing about them, what would it be? It's up to you as the storyteller to determine whether or not the character achieves the improvement. Both conditions can be useful depending on the theme of your story (recall the concept of positive and negative involvement).

From Tan's Tile - Tan needs to take more chances and think more creatively. He must recognize that the path to peace and harmony is not always through perfect order.

9. Explain the importance.

Explain why you consider this character important enough to include him or her in the story. If you don't find the character involving than no one else will either. List out the things you like about the character and the things that you don't like about the character. Force the character to defend his or her existence and inclusion in a story. Your characters work for you; you don't work for them.

From Tan's Tile - Tan is the central character in the story and through his over attention to order we learn about the theme of the power of creative thought.

10. *List potential interaction points.*

Outline the ways this character can interact with other character to create interesting situations and advance our understanding of the characters or the theme. This is your chance to play with the "what ifs" and is especially important for longer story structures or a series of smaller stories that feature recurring characters. You probably won't use many of the potential interaction points you invent, but almost every one should give you new insights into your characters.

From Tan's Tile - Tan interacts with his children as a father figure and his wife as a husband and partner. These interactions demonstrate his over emphasis on order and cause him to fail to make potential connections with the other characters.

Once you have answered each of these points for a character, review the information and descriptions you've recorded. Highlight key features and characteristics. From these highlights you should be able to develop a character profile. If not, revisit the ten points again to make sure you've fully explored all the possibilities.

If you still can't develop a character profile, the character is probably too weak to include in your story. In these cases it's best to shelve the character for a while and then revisit him or her at a later date.

Finding Good Characters

A natural alternative to creating your own characters is to simply find them in real life. (Stories that involve yourself, colleagues and/or friends almost always feature characters found in real life.) Everyone we meet is a potential character for our stories. More accurately, everyone we meet has potential qualities and characteristics we can use to build characters.

It's always better to adapt the interesting characteristics you find in people into new characters rather than simply dropping the people you know into a story. Simply including someone you know in a story can come back to haunt you. People may not approve of the way they are portrayed or may not like the very idea of being part of a story. If you're telling a story with a recognizable person as a character, chances are the news will travel back to them at some point.

Also, using an existing individual in a story as a character can actually limit the story. In most cases it's easier to explore the theme of the story by giving your characters aspects that play specific to that theme. For example, Tan's over-attention to maintaining order plays well into the story's theme of creative thought. Again, this is an example of a character with a negative relationship to the theme (It's also another example of repetition).

One trick is to combine the characteristics of two or more people to create a completely new character.

Creating a character completely from scratch takes a lot of creative energy. This also takes away energy from the other important elements of the story such as through line. This is another reason why many storytellers use the same core group of characters in every story they tell.

If you do borrow characters (or whole stories) from other people, always credit the original author. Also, never borrow a story for any purpose that directly leads to profit. For example, it's not fair to use a scene from a movie in a sales letter or have characters from a book push a product in a commercial. It also looks unimaginative and derivative.

Diversion: Character Studies

Think about your best friends. What qualities drew you to these people initially? What do you like best about them? What are their strengths? What are their weaknesses? If you were describing your best friend to another person, what would you say? Your answers to these questions describe who this person is as a character.

Although you would most likely never completely transcribe a personal friend into a story, considering these questions is an effective exercise in character development. The best characters are not unlike the people we know in real life.

In your story journal, write about an incident, event or occurrence that best sums up your relationship with your best friend.

7 Secrets

- Compelling characters are identifiable, involving and experience growth.
- Always invent a character backstory and determine core values.
- Describing a pivotal moment is an effective way of developing a character.
- It's helpful to compare and contrast characters with yourself.
- Introduce character strengths and weaknesses early in a story, not just when it is convenient to the plot.
- If you have trouble developing a character's full profile, the character may be too weak for the story.
- You can often adapt people in real life for use in stories.

Exercises

Fill in the Blanks

1. Compelling characters are _____, _____ and experience _____.

2. List the ten steps in character development:

a. _____

b. _____

c. _____

d. _____

e. _____

f. _____

g. _____

h. _____

i. _____

j. _____

Discussion Questions

1. Think about your favorite characters from books, movies and television. What makes each one a great character?

2. What types of qualities do you tend to remember most about a character?

Chapter 9 – Create a Through Line

Chapter Objectives

- Describe the two main types of through line and choose an appropriate type based on the goals of the program.
- Develop and maintain the through line within a story, linking it back to the theme of the story.
- Achieve a correct timing balance within the through line of a story.

Chapter Overview

The chapter explores the concept of through line within a story and introduces plot driven through lines and character driven through lines. It describes the pros and cons of each and provides guidance on when to use each type. The chapter also reviews the importance of timing within a story and explains how to achieve balance within a story.

Types of Through Lines

The through line describes the progression of action or dialog within a story. The pace of the through line is based on the structure of the story. An anecdote has a quick through line composed of only a few descriptive sentences or lines of dialog. A narrative through line follows the more established and gradual-paced three-act model.

There are two main types of through lines: plot-driven and character-driven.

Plot-driven

Plot-driven through lines are based on the events or actions within the story:

1. John goes to the store.
2. John buys a gallon of milk.
3. John returns home.
4. John has a bowl of cereal.
5. John discovers the milk was bad.
6. John looks at the expiration date.
7. John realizes he bought expired milk.

Plot-driven through lines tend to be more common because they are usually quicker and easier to construct. The actions above follow a natural course or linear path. Each section contains a clear link to the previous one. Although we could add in details such as John's conversation with the store clerk or a description of his cereal, the driving force in this story is the purchase of the milk and the discovery the milk is bad. The focus of this story is "what happened?"

The original *Law and Order* series by producer Dick Wolfe is an example of a plot-driven story. Each episode is concerned first and foremost with the crime at hand. Even though we may learn about the characters along the way, the crime investigation and subsequent trial drive the episode forward. We watch to see the result of the investigation and the verdict of the trial. It's a modern interpretation of the classic "whodunit" format.

Plot-driven through lines are more interesting when they break the pattern. The story above doesn't really get interesting until John discovers the milk is bad. If John simply takes the milk back and exchanges it for another one the story still isn't interesting (unless John himself is interesting). However, if John takes the expired milk and pours it over the clerk's head...now that's interesting. Again, John broke the pattern.

Character-driven

Character-driven through lines are based on the key characters within the story and how they react to events and other people. Character-driven through lines are generally more difficult to create because they do not have a built in linear path. A character-driven version of the "milk" story above would be more concerned with John's reaction to the spoiled milk or how he chose to deal with the situation. If John simply pours the milk down the sink and resolves to have toast instead of cereal, it tells us a lot about John.

The series *Law and Order: SVU* is an example of a character-driven story. Each episode is really a study of the various characters and how they react to the crime at hand. Through these reactions we learn more about the characters. In SVU episodes the crime is nearly always solved, but the solution is not as important as changes in the characters or new information we learn about them.

Because character-driven through lines are more complex and difficult to construct, many people automatically fall back on plot-driven through lines. You should never feel inadequate if you rely on plot as a through line. The majority of books, television and movies use this tried and true method. We have an innate fascination with events and actions and a desire to see "what happens next." Humans are naturally observant so all actions hold some degree of interest for us.

Character-driven through lines are more challenging to create because they require extremely interesting characters. We don't naturally find everyone around us naturally interesting. In fact, we tend to gravitate towards an inner circle of people we find most interesting.

The trade off is that when we do find another person or character interesting, that attention level is much stronger than the attention we pay to actions. Even though a character-driven through line is more difficult, it has the potential to strike a much deeper chord with your audience.

A further irony is that a plot-driven through line still requires characters at least partially interesting. However a character-driven through line can contain the most mundane plot imaginable. Even something as simple as buying a gallon of milk can hold our attention if the character buying the milk is interesting enough.

Imagine that before John picked out a gallon of milk, he insisted on taking every container out of the cooler in the store and lining them up according to date. Now John is a bit more interesting – primarily because he did something most of us do not do when picking out milk.

John broke a usual pattern and attracted our attention. The television series Monk is an example of a character-driven story.

It's also a twist on the "whodunit" format, but is more focused on the central character: Monk. We watch this series more to see how Monk will resolve the crime, rather than simply to see the crime solved.

Choosing a Through-line

Both the plot-driven through line and the character-driven through line can work with each of the structures, purposes and styles presented earlier in the book. They also perform equally well with different audience types and environments. Use your story's theme to determining whether to use a plot-driven or character-driven through line. Here are the general rules of thumb for choosing through line:

- Themes based on objects or goals work best with plot-driven through lines. Examples: making the big sale, the merits of a product or service, company history.
- Themes based on concepts or ideas work best with character-driven through lines. Examples: principles of leadership, job interview, values of the company founder.

There are always exceptions, but those rules are a good starting point. Let's take a product sales pitch as an example. If your product is unique or has qualities and advantages other products do not have, your theme is object-based. "Buy my product because it's better and cheaper."

If your product is a commodity and your commitment to customer service sets you apart from competition, your theme is concept-based. "Buy my product because the quality is just as good but I'll always give you better service."

In the first example, a plot-driven through line demonstrates the uniqueness and/or advantages of the product as it solves a specific problem for the customer. The story would be constructed from a series of actions or events resulting in the customer achieving a specific goal (such as surviving a car crash or cleaning off a tough stain).

In the second example, a character-driven through line would demonstrate the commitment to service constructed from the interaction between a company representative and the customer.

Let's look at another example. If you're telling a friend how you finally mastered the hardest hole of the golf course the through line is plot-driven. You are describing a means to an end. If you're telling a potential employer the same story but to demonstrate you don't give up until you get something right the through-line would be character-driven.

By the way, don't forget about audience analysis. You would probably only want to use the golf story if you knew for sure the potential employer played golf.

In the first instance the story is about the goal. In the second instance the story is about you as a person (a character). The same story can be constructed in multiple ways to achieve different themes.

Converting a plot-driven story into a character-driven story and vise versa is a good way to double your story inventory. There are all sorts of ways to change the perspective of your stories and make them applicable to different situations and themes.

Maintaining a Through line

The best way to maintain a through line is through planning and story structure. Unnecessary tangents and sidebars can distract the audience and break their concentration, especially in a verbal setting. You're always free to experiment with different organizational techniques but it's generally best to stay close to the standard three-act format.

This is particularly true for educational and motivational purposes. The nature of entertaining and inspirational stories allows some leeway.

A degree of planning is necessary for any story. The amount of planning varies based on three key factors:

Length – Longer story structures, especially narratives, require more planning. At the least you'll need a full and often detailed outline for longer stories. Without an exact plan you're likely to stray into tangents and bury your theme.

Formality – More preparation is necessary for formal environments and audiences. Also, several story types require greater formality. The mythical style requires more planning because these stories tend to deal with deeper themes, characters and plots.

Importance – The more important the story, the greater the preparation (regardless of structure). A sixty-second television commercial is structurally an anecdote, but because the ad is a significant part of the business model (and usually high cost) it's extremely important and requires a high degree of preparation.

At this point you may be asking: What about spontaneity? It's true you never want any of your stories to sound "canned" or resemble the a political candidate's stump speech. Ideally you want your stories to appear natural and unrehearsed. Planning and practice earn you the right to spontaneity. Your improvised comments and reactions only add to the story if you've prepared beforehand.

A humorous comment made in the spur of the moment may get a large laugh, but also may be distracting to the audience if it doesn't relate back to the theme of the story. The best stand-up comedians always sound as if they're saying or doing something for the first time. Most comedians practice and fine tune their routines many times, though.

A solid, well-practiced through line makes it easier for you to improvise and adapt. It allows you to always know where you've been, where you're at and where you're going within the story. That allows you to interject comments and reactions without derailing the story.

In most cases, outlining is the easiest and most effective way to plan and practice a story. An outline provides an "at a glance" view of the story and allows you to quickly scan different levels of detail. Outlines are also completely scalable. An anecdote may only have a few top-level bullets points. Episodes may have two to three levels of detail and a narrative more than three. Outlines are also effective in situations where you can use notes when delivering your story.

Another method is to completely write out the story. This method is usually based on an outline (so an outline is always a good place to start). Any story that requires some type of production or staging is usually written out or scripted. A script or transcript of a story is a good way to capture all the details. It works particularly well for stories that should be repeated in the same way each time (or by multiple people).

Storyboarding is another effective method of story planning, but generally requires special skills or expensive software. Unfortunately, in order for a storyboard to be effective, you must have some drawing ability. Stick figures are helpful to determine physical placement (called blocking) and some motion, but only convey the most basic interactions and feelings.

Timing

I'm sure you've heard the old saying that "timing is everything." That concept probably has roots in storytelling. In both oral and written stories timing (and the timeline) is the most important aspect of through line. Have you ever sat through a movie that seemed to move too slow? Or one that moved so fast you couldn't follow the story? Did you ever listen to a speaker who took long, seemingly unnatural pauses between sentences or phrases?

These are all mistakes of timing. The most common example of the importance of timing is humor. Abbott and Costello's "Who's on First?" routine works because of the quick banter between the two men. Neither has a chance to realize the disagreement in semantics. Likewise, the audience scarcely has a chance to recover from one laugh before another one comes along.

This type of quick wit is often used to describe the importance of timing. However, a longer pause can be just as powerful. In one episode of Matt Groening's animated television show *The Simpsons*, Homer Simpson decides to start his own internet company. His first customer is a round, nerdy fellow known only as "Comic Book Guy."

Comic Book Guy asks Homer a question about his service loaded with techno-speak any non-computer expert would have trouble understanding (let alone the often dim-witted yet well meaning Homer). Homer stares at Comic Book Guy blankly for several seconds, before replying: "Can I have some money now?" That long pause is the right timing for that scene.

Each scene in a story may have its own timing requirements. The timing of these individual scenes adds up to form acts and eventually the entire through line. It can get relatively complex, especially in a larger story structure. Many times the correct timing for a scene is simply "what feels right." This implies the need for practice when telling stories. Until you read or say a scene out loud it can be difficult to find the correct timing.

Timing both within scenes and between scenes is all a matter of balance. For example, in the narrative three-act structure it's common for the first and third act to be half as long as the second act. Two long scenes in a row can be balanced out by a shorter scene. The "dot and dash system" as it's sometimes called is used to analyze balance in a story. Short scenes are represented by dots and long scenes are represented by dashes. A three act narrative might look like this:

| . - - . - ...- | -..-.--.--..-..--.- | ..-.---..-..- |

The story above would be considered to have a good balance of shorter and longer scenes with each of the three main acts as well as the overall relationship of the acts to each other. In most cases, if the scenes and acts are balanced the story itself is well balanced.

The Right Through Line

The right through line is a combination of three main elements:

- Choosing the right type of through line based on the theme.
- Developing a compelling set of actions, events and/or characters.
- Developing the right balance and timing throughout acts and scenes.

Often the through line of a story is relegated to a simple outline or plot summary. To compare building a story to building a house, the through line is similar to the main beams that hold the house together. The most important elements in the through line such as key events or pivotal dialog are the load-bearing walls of the house. If the base structure of the house isn't sound, it doesn't matter what picture you hang on the wall.

The quest for the right through line naturally flows into the construction of acts and scenes, covered in depth in the next chapter.

Diversion: Timing is Everything

As mentioned in this chapter, timing is important to any story and especially important in humor. Timing can make or break a stand up comedy routine or humorous scene in a television show or movie. To see timing in action, attend a stand up comedy show, skit show or comedy play. As an alternative, watch comedic television shows or movies.

As you watch, record the timing elements as dots and dashes. Use dots to denote shorter bits and dashes to denote longer bits. After watching, review the dots and dashes and use your story journal to reflect on the timing. Look for patterns and balance. Compare these points to the parts of the routine or show that received the biggest laughs. You should see a pattern.

7 Secrets

- Choose the through line for your story based on the theme of your story.
- Plot-driven through lines are useful for themes based on objects or goals.
- Character-driven through lines are useful for themes based on concepts or ideas.
- Character-driven through lines are usually more difficult to create but often provide more lasting results.
- Some degree of planning is necessary for any story, but varies based on the length, formality and importance.
- Timing is one of the most important elements in any story.
- Always maintain a balance of short and long scenes in a story.

Exercises

Fill in the Blanks

1. The two types of through line are _____ and _____.

2. Themes based on objects or goals work best with _____ through lines.

3. Themes based on concepts or ideas work best with _____ through lines.

4. The amount of through line planning depends on three key elements: _____, _____ and _____.

5. Timing between scenes is a matter of _____.

Discussion Questions

1. What are the advantages and disadvantages of the two types of through lines? How can you capitalize on the advantages and overcome the disadvantages?

2. What are some strategies for managing timing in written stories? How can you control the rate or pace at which the reader experiences the story?

Chapter 10 – Add Acts and Scenes

Chapter Objectives

- Plan the development of your stories based on a structure of acts and scenes.
- Use parallel construction to maintain continuity between scenes.
- Recognize the practice of reading and telling stories to improve your own ability.

Chapter Overview

The chapter reviews the development of through line in a story using acts and scenes to build the structure piece by piece. It also focuses on the importance of parallel construction within stories and explains how to use this technique on several levels including within your stories.

Breaking Stories Down

The previous chapter on through line introduced the concepts of acts and scenes within a story. The degree to which acts and scenes are recognizable depends on the structure of the story. An anecdote may very well have only one act and one scene. Episodes and narratives have acts and scenes clearly delineated by a major event (usually referred to as a plot point). In television, the end of each act is also followed by a series of commercials.

Because humans process information in bits and bites, it's always necessary to break your message (and stories) down into smaller components. Stories should generally be three to five points and never more than seven. That's why most stories have only three acts and generally never more than five.

Would you want to sit through a seven-act play? More complex stories or messages should be broken down into three to five major points, each of which contains several sub-points.

In stories, acts are the main points. Scenes are the sub-points. Here is an outline of the acts and scenes in "Tan's Tile":

1. Tan Breaks a Tile
    a. Tan is placing tiles in his garden.
    b. Tan drops the last tile and it breaks.
2. Tan Tries to Fix the Tile
    a. Tan arranges the pieces as a swan (wife notices).
    b. Tan arranges the pieces as a fox (son notices).
    c. Tan arranges the pieces as a cat (daughter notices).
3. Tan Recreates the Square

    a. Tan finally arranges the pieces in a square.

    b. No one notices his square.

Because "Tan's Tile" is an anecdote, its outline is much shorter and the acts and scenes run together. Also, the size ratios between the acts are not as pronounced. The middle act still holds the majority of the content, though.

The typical three-act structure usually contains two plot points. Plot points are major events within a story. A plot point marks a significant change within the direction of the plot or the development of a character. The first plot point occurs just at the end of the first act and the second plot point occurs just at the end of the second act.

Acts

In most cases the three acts of a story represent the beginning, middle and end. Applied to traditional speaking methods: In act one you "tell them what you're going to tell them." In act two you "tell them." In act three you "tell them what you've told them." The main difference in storytelling is that you're using metaphor and example to do the telling.

Examine your theme to determine what should happen in the first, second and third act:

- The first act typically sets up the theme.
- The second act contains a series of challenges or events that demonstrate the theme.
- The third act reiterates the theme.

The main character should always experience a sense of growth regarding the theme. A young salesman learns to handle a difficult client. An old fisherman learns a few new tricks from his young nephew. Without this growth of the central character the theme can fall flat and the audience left wondering about the point of the story.

The first act of Tan's Tile sets up the conditions of the story. Tan is working in the garden. He has only one tile left. He drops the last tile and it breaks. Tan decides to try and put the tile back together. He tries to reform the tile back into a square; he's literally thinking "in the box" at this point. This is an example of setting up theme through contrast or "reversal" and is a good way to establish character growth.

In the second act Tan tries to recreate the square several times but only manages to create shapes resembling animals. A member of his family notices each time he creates a shape. Tan stubbornly continues to recreate the square. Repetition is a common technique of demonstrating theme with the second act. In a longer story, repetition is often followed by incremental growth in the main character.

There are generally three ways of handling repetition:

- A series of lessons through failures
- A period of growth by overcoming challenges
- A combination of the two.

A balance of setbacks and successes is especially affective for longer stories and is common in most books, movies and television shows. Another variation on the combined technique is to provide a steady series of successes followed by a major setback. (Remember that balance is the key to a good through line.)

Tan's Tile offers a twist on this idea. Tan creates several animal shapes that please his family. (He just doesn't see these as successes in the moment.) His major setback is actually when he creates the square. This occurs in the third act. We can only hope he sees the error of his ways. This type of implied change is more common in older story forms such as the legend on which Tan's Tile is based.

Most modern stories contain a much more concrete demonstration of resolution. The conclusion is not left up to the reader. More creative endeavors afford the freedom to use a more subtle resolution. However, business applications of storytelling require a clear statement of the resolution (in most cases the call to action).

Reversal, repetition and resolution provide a three-part strategy for storytelling:

- Reversal - Set up the reversal of your theme in act one by demonstrating some type of contract between the current situation and the correct situation.
- Repetition - Demonstrate repetition of the theme in act two by showing characters working through a series of events or challenges.
- Resolution - In act three provide the resolution (and usually a restatement) of the theme.

Scenes

The number of scenes in a story varies widely depending on the structure. The most common delineation between scenes is based on a change in a location or a significant change in time. By this definition Tan's Tile only has one scene per act. Each of the smaller exchanges or events happens within the same event and immediately one after the other. There is a slight time lapse between acts as Tan tries to recreate the square.

Even though scenes are smaller units, each contains a beginning, middle and an end. In act two of Tan's Tile, Tan creates several shapes from the broken tile. Each of these little scenes follows a specific rhythm: Tan creates the shape, a member of his family comments on it and Tan gets more frustrated with his inability to recreate the square. This common rhythm maintains continuity through the scenes.

Parallel Construction

This rhythm is an example of parallel construction. There are several other techniques for producing continuity. Re-use of a common or catch phrase is one easy method. More subtle methods involve re-use of symbols or colors. However, parallel construction is by far the best method. The scenes in act two are an example of "physical" or "structural" parallel construction.

On a structural level, parallel construction repeats the same grammatical elements in the same order throughout a story:

1. Tan arranged the pieces to form a swan. His wife was pleased.
2. Tan arranged the pieces to form a fox. His son was pleased.

3. Tan arranged the pieces to form a cat. His daughter was pleased.
4. Tan arranged the pieces to form a square. No one noticed.

The contrast in the final sentence makes the pattern "pop" the same way green shutters on a yellow house make it pop in terms of its curb appeal. The parallel structure in this case is:

Subject	Past Tense Verb	Object	Infinitive	Object
Tan	arranged	the pieces	to form	a cat.

Although this example re-uses the same exact word, you can achieve parallel construction simply by repeating the same parts of speech in the same order:

Wong kneaded the dough to create a loaf. Tan was pleased.

Subject	Past Tense Verb	Object	Infinitive	Object
Wong	Kneaded	the dough	to create	a loaf.

Here's a more business-related example:

1. We tried lowering the price. The client still didn't sign.
2. We tried adding more resources. The client still didn't sign.

3. We tried a new approach. The client agreed to consider it.

Structural parallel construction is generally easier to initiate and maintain. It allows you to fall back on a concise model and instantly provides a flow and rhythm to your stories. Used properly it can give the story an almost lyric quality. Mythical stories especially benefit from this format.

Symbolic Parallel Construction

Now imagine for the moment Tan left the broken tile behind and went to bake some bread. There is a mishap in the kitchen and the bread fails to rise. Tan's son points out the flat bread would go well with a relish the family likes but Tan is still disappointed with the bread. Tan is essentially dissatisfied with both the broken tile and the flat bread for the same reason: it does not fit his high ideal.

Symbolic, metaphorical and thematic-based parallel constructions is more difficult but can produce a richer story overall. Sometimes we are lucky enough to find stories naturally containing these parallels. This is the "truth is stranger" than fiction phenomenon.

Think about your favorite personal story – the one you tell all the time. It might be a story about how you met your spouse, the time you won a big account or the funny thing that happened on last year's vacation. Why is this story your favorite? What are the common themes and elements running through each part of the story?

Those common themes and elements (the same characteristics that make the story great) provide the parallel construction. The tricky part is that thematic-based parallel construction can easily become forced and mechanical. For that reason there really is no model for creating this type of common thread between your scenes. However, you can ask the following questions about every scene in your story:

1. How does this scene relate to the theme?
2. Why is this scene important to the story?
3. What is the transition between the previous scene and this one? This one and the next?
4. What actions or dialog takes place that is similar to that in other scenes?
5. How does this scene reflect other scenes in the story?
6. How is this scene the culmination of everything that came before it?
7. How does this scene add to the eventual resolution at the end of the story?

After asking these questions, you may find that a scene simply does not belong.

Importance of Practice

Every time you hear or read a story your own affinity for storytelling grows a bit. That's why the best writers are usually avid readers. The more stories you encounter, the more you'll recognize the patterns within them and the similarities they have to each other.

The historical documentaries mentioned earlier in the book are a particularly good source. These documentaries make dry topics interesting and make a lot out of a little. There's also nothing like experiencing a story first hand. If the storyteller is accessible, ask them about their own creative process.

Look for opportunities to practice storytelling, both socially and at work. The best storytellers use stories in multiple aspects of their lives. You'll gain a better sense of what works in specific situations. Parallel construction and other techniques become almost second nature.

Another method of practicing is to try telling other people's stories. This is an excellent way to recognize parallel construction and observe how others weave acts and scenes together. Stay true to the original story and format at first. Once you get comfortable with the story, try telling it your own way. Here are some exercises:

- Use Tan's Tile to illustrate creative thinking at work.
- Re-tell a Shakespearian play using a journalistic style.
- Ask a friend to tell you their most embarrassing moment and then re-tell it to them. (Allow them to do the same for you.)
- Interview a married couple and write a mythical story based on how they met.
- Relate an episode of your favorite one-hour television drama as an anecdote.
- Rewrite your company's corporate history in your own words. (Feel free to be humorous.)
- Think of the worst movie you've ever seen and imagine how you would have written the story.

A common theme in all of the exercises above is the conversion of a story from one type to another. It's like taking the story apart and putting it back together again – but in a new way. The act of converting a story from one structure, purpose and style to another can provide a lot of insight into what makes a story work.

Storytelling is innate and universal. As you tell more stories you'll reawaken the natural instinct all humans have for storytelling.

Diversion: Your Favorite Stories

What is your favorite movie? How about your favorite television show? Your diversion for this chapter is to watch each of them. However, this time watch closely for the divisions between acts and scenes. Answer the following questions:

- Does the movie or television show follow the traditional three-act structure? If not, what is the structure?
- What is the major plot point at the end of act one? Act two?
- How do the writer and/or director transition the movie or show between scenes?
- Is there a regular rhythm of longer scenes and shorter scenes?
- What parallel structures run throughout the movie or show? What parallels run through sequels or the show series?

Review your answers and consider how these strategies contribute to the success of the story. List ways you can apply these same strategies in your own stories.

7 Secrets

- All stores are broken down into acts and scenes.
- All stories and individual scenes have a beginning, middle and end.
- The basic three-act structure with plot points at the end of the first and second act is a good model for storytelling.
- There are three ways to handle repetition: a series of lessons through failures and growth by overcoming challenges or a combination of the two.
- Reversal, repetition and resolution are a three-part strategy for constructing acts and scenes.
- Parallel construction ties acts and scenes together and links them back to the theme.
- Parallel construction can be structural or symbolic.

Exercises

Fill in the Blanks

1. In most cases the three acts of a story represent the
_____, _____ and
_____.

2. List the three ways of handling repetition:

a. _____

b. _____

c. _____

3. A three-part strategy for storytelling includes
_____, _____ and
_____.

4. List the two types of parallel construction:

a. _____

b. _____

4. One of the best ways to become a better storyteller is
_____.

Discussion Questions

1. Do all stories have to follow the traditional three-act structure? Why or why not? What additional challenges do you face as a storyteller when not using the three-act structure?

2. How can you use parallel structure in your every day speech? How might this affect your message?

Part 3: Story Implementation

Chapter 11: Example Stories

Chapter Objectives:

- Examine an implementation of storytelling through two specific examples.
- Review how the various story components come together to convey a specific message.
- Generate your own ideas for practical storytelling.

Chapter Overview

In this chapter we'll explore the various parts of story through two examples. Each uses stories to convey specific messages. The final projects are available at www.practicalstorytelling.com.

Introduction

To demonstrate how story components come together, let's look at two specific examples: An online training program on Effective Writing and a marketing campaign for a fictional museum. Links to the finished products are presented at the beginning of each example. In order to provide robust examples, I chose an online training program and a museum brochure. The nature of these formats prevented me from including them directly in the book. Therefore I've published both examples online.

It's recommended that you begin each example by viewing the final product. Then review each step and how it relates to the finished product. After each example are completed worksheets. Appendix B also contains a series of short example stories.

Example 1: Effective Writing eLearning Program

Finished product:
http://www.praticalstorytelling.com/writing

Determine the theme

Teach principles that produce more effective writing in a relatively short time. Effective writing is a large topic. However, in this case we have identified a specific need: address three key areas that can produce a noticeable improvement in business writing in a short period of time (2 to 3 weeks of practice). We've whittled down a potentially large topic into a smaller, more manageable one.

The theme derives from specific motivations: 1) Help people identify common and ongoing problems with their writing. 2) Provide strategies to improve your writing within a relatively short amount of time.

Analyze the audience

People writing in an "everyday" business setting. We can breakdown information about the audience using the BEARS technique:

- Background – Business professions with varying positions within training, sales and marketing fields.
- Ethnicity – Varied, with the implication being that slang, jargon and euphuisms should be avoided.
- Age – Approximately 25-55.
- Relationships – Relationships are not as directly important in an online program because it is usually a single-user medium. However the interactive relationship between the audience and the program must be considered. The program should anticipate questions and issues.
- Skills – People will enter the program with varying degrees of writing skill; probably looking for tips in different areas. The implication is that this program must allow the audience to quickly branch to their specific areas of interest.

For larger programs, you would conduct a more in-depth audience analysis. This example also demonstrates why it is often easier to delivery a program that is more tailored to a specific audience.

Develop the through line

This program has three key areas of through line:

- There is an instructional through line that examines the improvement of a single paragraph example throughout the program.
- Both this paragraph and the program relate to a comic strip running throughout all the training programs in this series.
- The program runs in an interface template used repeatedly in all the programs in a series of courses on basic business skills.

Introduce characters

A themed comic strip runs throughout the program. The characters in the strip work on the example paragraph revised within the chapter. Although they are animals, the characters are "consultants" working with another firm on a project. Most people can identify with the characters, since we've all either been or worked with consultants at one time or another.

Divide into acts and scenes

The program contains three sections: grammatical guide, writing process and writing strategies. These three sections are further sub-divided into specific topics within each. Individual screens in the program breakdown the material presented into a number of lists, bullet points, definitions and steps.

Example 2: Liberty Heritage Museum Brochure: Pathways to Adventure Program

Finished product:
http://www.practicalstorytelling.com/liberty

Determine the theme

Motivate local organizations to host artifacts from the Liberty Heritage Museum's collection at their facility to provide adventure, intrigue, culture and education to the community. Because we have a specific theme in mind, we know exactly what story our marketing piece must tell and how to judge its success. The theme derives from two problems the museum faces:

- It doesn't have enough room to display its entire collection.
- It seeks to strengthen its relationship with the community.

Analyze the audience

We can breakdown information about the audience using the BEARS technique:

- Background – CEO and VP level individuals in metro area businesses. Early analysis also excluded the target audience based on yearly revenue. However, upon review we realized smaller businesses could partner to host museum collections.
- Ethnicity – Varied, so the campaign should appeal to various cultural backgrounds. This is

achieved by including pieces from several different collections in the brochure.

- Age – Approximately 40-60.
- Relationships – Many of these individuals and organizations already support other museums and the arts in the metro area. They also have strong ties and economic influence on the community.
- Skills – These individuals have in excess of 15 years experience in the business world. They understand the importance of concepts such as return on investment and public relations. The skills and background in this case tell us the brochure is only the start of the campaign. The brochure should either be hand delivered or followed-up by a personal visit. An "open house" at the museum with cocktails and Hors D'Oeuvres is also included.

In this case, we are working with a specific target audience. This allows us to tailor the message to that audience.

Develop the through line

The main elements of through line in this brochure are the theme of adventure and the concept of a "pathway." A visual pathway via footprints runs throughout the brochure and "leads" the audience from section to section.

Introduce characters

In this case we're casting the audience directly as a character, challenging them to pursue adventure, intrigue culture and education with the museum program.

Divide into acts and scenes

The brochure is sectioned in several ways. There are four main areas:

- The headline panel (the first panel you see based on the fold). This area has one goal: attract attention.
- The inside panel (created when the brochure is completely unfolded). This area contains most of the content and is designed to achieve retention.
- The contact panel (opposite of the headline panel when the brochure is folded). This area delivers the specific information needed to affect behavior (or create permission for a museum representative to make contact.)
- The back panels (two panels "left over" after the headline and contact panel). These provide supplemental information.

Diversion: Breaking it into Bits

Humans process information in bits (or pieces) of three to five, and never more than seven. Consider social security numbers. Almost everyone can remember his or her social security number because:

- It has three main sections (xxx-xx-xxxx).
- Each section has a different length.
- No section has a length longer than 4.

This book is broken down into three parts, each of which contains five chapters. Where else have you seen a similar pattern? See if you can spot other instances where information is broken down into sets of three to five bits.

7 Secrets

- Stories contain five main components: theme, audience analysis, through line, characters and acts and scenes.
- Theme is the central element of all stories.
- Audience analysis is one of the most important components of any story.
- Consider audience analysis when developing the other components of a story.
- People process information in bits of 3 to 5, and never more than 7.
- Always break down the information in your story.
- The Story Design Worksheet can be used to develop and record the components of a story.

Exercises

Discussion Questions

1. What common elements do each of the examples in this chapter share? Why do they share each of these elements?

2. How does each of these examples employ the various elements parts of a story differently to achieve their respective goals?

3. What strategies does each of these stories use to connect with the specific audience? How could they be more effective?

4. Both of these examples are written stories. How do written stories differ from spoken stories? How you modify each of these stories to present them to a live audience?

5. How would you contract or shorten each of these stories if forced to present them in a shorter timeframe? For example, how would you present the Effective Writing campaign in 20 minutes or 10 PowerPoint slides? How would you present the Museum program in a postcard, flyer, poster or direct mail letter?

Chapter 12 – Factoring the Environment

Chapter Objectives

- Analyze the environment in which you'll be delivering your story according to physical conditions, current events and overall atmosphere.
- Develop strategies to overcome the challenges of the environment and factor them into your story.

Chapter Overview

This chapter discusses the effect the environment can have on a story. It describes methods of determining the environment before you delivery your story, as well as ways to observe the environment while delivering the story. The chapter also lists several strategies to overcome specific environmental problems.

Importance of Environment

No story exists in a vacuum. In addition to the demographics and psychographics of the audience, the overall environment also affects how a story is interpreted. A corporate motivational speech takes on quite a different feel depending on the current health of the company. The environment can almost become an additional audience member.

A negative environment can even become a heckler, drawing attention and energy away from your story. A badly performing company or a team under a tight deadline can draw down energy. Audience members continually devote a portion of their energy toward thinking or worrying about those events. This is another demonstration of Maslow's Hierarhy of Needs.

That said, it is also possible the environment may be neutral enough to have an insignificant effect. For example, if you're telling a story to prove a point during the course of a routine business meeting, chances are the environment won't be as much of a factor. However, it is best to consider each of these elements – especially for more important stories.

Three aspects make up the environment of a story: physical conditions, current events and overall atmosphere.

Physical conditions

Description

Physical conditions are the most common aspect of environment. The first part of this book reviewed the way temperature can affect an audience. A room that is too hot or too cold can make it difficult for an audience to concentrate. Almost any adverse physical condition can quickly become an issue: too small of a room for the group size, uncomfortable chairs, audio/visual problems, etc.

The tricky part of physical conditions is they are not always immediately evident. For example, a speaker may not immediately notice the room is too small as long as his or her podium area is sufficient. Audio/visual elements almost always cause problems – even when the storyteller prepares beforehand. Look for the following possible conditions:

- Room too hot
- Room too cold
- Room too small
- Room too big
- Individuals too crowded together
- Uncomfortable seating
- Audience unable to hear
- Speaker too loud
- Distracting outside noises
- Distracting windows or artwork
- Room to bright or too dark
- Distracting elements of the speaker's dress

All of these items seem superficial at first, but they can have a significant affect on a story. A laundry detergent company demonstrated this with a popular commercial. In the commercial a job applicant had a stain on his shirt. Every time he opened his mouth to answer a question, the stain would yell out non-sense phrases. Although a bit silly, the commercial makes a valid a point. Chances are good the stain would distract the interviewer.

Strategies

In many cases a problem with the physical conditions can be fixed with a twist of the thermostat or switch to another room. However, there are times when you have no control over the physical conditions. If you're at a client location it's likely you'll have limited control over the environment.

In these cases you must adapt to the conditions. This first step is to take a moment and assess the physical conditions before beginning the story. You can't necessary start by asking if everyone is hot or cold, or has a comfortable seat. But you can scope the room out beforehand (in most cases).

There are three steps to dealing with physical conditions:

1. Assess the situation.
2. Determine whether or not you have control.
3. Fix or adapt based on the degree of control.

Look for any of the conditions listed above. If you spot an item that could be a problem, determine whether or not you can control the element. If you can control the element, simply change it to be more favorable. If you cannot control the element causing the problem, you will have to adapt to the situation. Consider the following adaptation strategies:

- Shorten your story by dropping details
- Tell your story more slowly and deliberately
- Postpone the story to a later date
- Add more humor to your story
- Ask for audience feedback more frequently
- Draw the distracting factor into your story

If all else fails, the last suggestion above (draw the distracting factor into your story) can be very effective. Our first instinct is often to simply ignore the problem. This is difficult for both the speaker and the audience. A better strategy is to openly acknowledge the element and work it into your story.

For example, if the room is too hot make a joke in the story about the characters being too hot. If there is something unusual just outside a window, have one of the characters discover it. This method minimizes the distracting element by making it into something humorous and provides the audience with a direct connection to the story.

Current events

Description

Current events include external and internal events. External events are basically everything you see on the evening news (including the weather). Internal events are specific to the audience.

If a company is facing the possibility of bankruptcy, that's a very local event that directly affects any story told within that environment. Just like a room that's too hot, you cannot simply ignore this fact. A corporate motivation speech that does not acknowledge the company's current position (in a realistic way) is sure to fail.

Events can happen on a multitude of levels and there's no way to ultimately know about every single one. It's possible there are different events affecting each individual within your audience. It's not as much of an issue with a smaller audience but multiply this by thousands or even millions and you can start to understand how hard it can be to put together an effective television commercial.

Not only must you reach the correct target demographic, the target must be in the correct frame of mind to receive the message. The trick in this case is to simply "play the numbers." If you hit enough people some of them are statistically likely to be in the right frame of mind to receive your message. Repeat the same message multiple times and eventually you'll get a critical mass of people in the right frame of mind.

Strategies

Use the following steps to analyze and adapt to current events:

1. Describe the situation. Taking a few minutes to write a summary of the current situation can help you better understand it. Make sure you examine all sides of the event. List all the affected parties and indicate how the situation impacts them specifically.

2. Determine the possible impact. Based on your description, list all the possible ways the event can affect your audience. Address as many of these impacts as you can within the story and specifically within the theme.

3. Acknowledge the situation. Never try to ignore current events when delivering a story. If a team has been experiencing disagreements, acknowledge that fact when delivering your story. Unless your story is designed for purely entertainment, you don't have the luxury of subtlety. Your audience should clearly draw the connection between the current event and the theme.

4. Connect the situation to the theme. Based on the description you wrote above, map the conditions of the situation to theme of your story. (If you have difficulty doing so, the theme of your story may need to be modified.) Once the audience understands the theme of the story, it should provide them with a new strategy for dealing with the current events. If the group can't get past disagreements, use compromise as the theme of your story.

Overall Atmosphere

Description

The atmosphere is often the least apparent of the three elements, but it can also be the most detrimental. This is especially true in cases when the audience doesn't really want to be there. Training classes face this issue on at least a semi-regular basis. Most audiences are too polite to simply say: "We don't really want to be here." You'll have to deduce these types of situations when they occur.

There are a lot of reasons why someone would not want to listen to your story - most of them are not a direct reflection on you. It could be they have something else to do, they are pre-occupied with another problem, or it's simply a nice day outside. You also inherit the atmosphere of your setting.

If you're in a three hour-long business meeting, chances are people will be tired and distracted if your story is not the very first thing they hear. In the case of a television commercial the audience would rather be watching the show. We read newspapers and magazines to read the articles and not the ads (most of the time).

In any case it all adds up to the same thing: the audience would rather be somewhere else or doing something else. Body language and other non-verbal cues are the best way to gauge the overall atmosphere of your audience. Look for the following negative non-verbal cues to indicate a poor overall atmosphere:

- Lack of eye contact
- Blank stare
- Chatting among themselves
- Sighing
- Crossed arms
- Doodling
- Rubbing back of the neck
- Eye rolls
- Throat clearing
- General fidgeting
- Rubbing eyes or face

Keep in mind all of these gestures could also mean your story isn't interesting or isn't establishing a connection with the audience. Examine your story and be honest with yourself about whether the overall atmosphere is due to the original feelings of the audience or the effect of your story.

Strategies

There are several ways to turnaround a negative atmosphere. One of the easiest and most common is the use of an icebreaker. An icebreaker can be as simple as an opening joke or as complex as a fifteen-minute audience activity. An icebreaker can help people temporarily forget their previous attitude and shift the frame of reference. By shifting their frame of reference, the icebreaker indicates to the audience they are about to experience something different.

Here are some icebreaker ideas:

- Short joke (choose something appropriate to the situation)
- Traditional story opening (once upon a time, a long time ago, etc.)
- Audience polling (how many of you have...)
- Open-ended question (what was your best sales experience...)
- Individual activity (design your own vanity license plate...)
- Group activity (design a customer service crest for our company...)

These are just some overall suggestions. There are many other books with icebreaker activities. You can also find many free suggestions on the Internet. Icebreakers aren't just for the beginning of the story. They can also be a quick and easy way to snap back the interest of your audience. Always tie your icebreaker back to your theme if possible.

Environment and Story Elements

Environment and the Theme

Theme is the area most often in conflict with the environment. The theme of your story is often set well before the environment. In most cases you'll have to adapt to manage the theme with the environment. Since the theme is the core, unifying element of your story, it's not recommended you try to modify the theme based on the environment.

However, you can consider how the theme relates to the environment and try to cover that within the content of the story. You can also pick out specific aspects of the environment that relate to the theme. For example, if the room is too hot it can serve as a metaphor for the heated arguments within a group. A room that is too cold can also symbolize the coldness group members feel towards each other.

Environment and the Characters

Try to relate your characters to the environment of the story whenever possible. Some characters may simply be inappropriate for the environment. In the previous case of the company in trouble, animated or exaggerated characters may not be the best choice. However, in the case of the group plagued by disagreements these types of characters may be exactly the right choice.

One of the most important training programs on groups and meetings was actually created by the Jim Henson Company and features the Muppets. People often get a "reality check" when they see exaggerated versions of themselves and others.

Environment and the Through Line

The environment has its greatest effect on the pacing of the through line. As previously mentioned, the pacing of your story is mainly about balance. Outside influences from the environment can throw off this balance. For example, if the audience becomes distracted it can derail your forward progress through the story.

Shorter scenes can become longer as you struggle to maintain the audience's attention. Try to build some flexibility into your pace to account for problems with the environment.

Environment and the Audience

Environment works best when coupled with audience analysis (covered in a separate chapter). Stories always work best when told within the context of the audience and environment around them. One method of interpreting literature is actually to remove the story entirely from the context of the time period and the author's biography. Although this is often useful and insightful from an academic standpoint, it's not as effective in practical storytelling.

Diversion: A Titan Among Men

In the movie *Remember the Titans*, Denzel Washington plays high school football coach Herman Boone. Boone is hired to coach the team in 1971 after the initiation of busing into the local school system. He faces resentment from the local community as he struggles to pull together black and white students into a cohesive team. Matters are further complicated with the presence of the former head coach with a style that's radically different than Boone's.

The movie offers a compelling and uncompromising look into a turbulent time. Washington's character struggles to tell his story of teamwork and disciplined football in an environment that can only be described as extremely hostile. In addition, the movie itself succeeded in an environment with a plethora of football movies and sports movies in general.

When people talk about *Remember the Titans*, they often mention how they were reluctant to go see "yet another sports movie." However, most were pleasantly surprised. The movie demonstrates on multiple levels how a story can succeed in a difficult environment.

7 Secrets

- The environment can have a significant effect on your story, even acting as an additional audience member.
- There are three aspects to environment: physical, current events and the overall atmosphere.
- The first step in dealing with environment is to assess the situation.
- You can't always control the environment, but you can often adapt.
- Continually gauge the audience and their body language.
- An icebreaker is a good way to capture the audience's attention and shift their focus.
- Environment affects each element of your story in a specific way.

Exercises

Fill in the Blanks

1. The three components that make up the environment are _____, _____ and _____.

2. List the four strategies of analyzing and adapting to current events:

a. _____

b. _____

c. _____

d. _____

3. Always tie your icebreaker back to your _____.

Discussion Questions

1. What are some strategies for examining the environment prior to telling a story?

2. How can you tailor your story if the environment changes shortly before delivery?

3. Are there any environments that are simply not compatible with storytelling? Why or why not?

Chapter 13 – Finding Stories

Chapter Objectives

- Collect stories from various sources and record them in a story journal.
- Match stories to specific themes according to the SMART parameters.
- Locate sources of good stories.

Chapter Overview

This chapter reviews the various places you can find good stories and the importance of keeping a story journal. It explains how to match the stories you find to specific themes according to the SMART parameters: specific, measurable, attainable, relevant and timely.

Collecting Stories

Finding stories isn't necessarily difficult. The challenge is finding the right story to go with the specific situation. The first step is collecting as many good stories as you can from different sources. Your initial focus should be whether or not the story attracts and holds your attention. It's difficult to always know exactly when or why you might use a story. It may be weeks, months or even years before you have a use for a story. The best storytellers collect stories as a lifetime quest.

It is hard to make up a story for a specific purpose. It's even harder to make up a story for a specific purpose and have it sound natural and spontaneous. That's why it's so important to collect stories as you hear or experience them.

Don't limit yourself to stories that happen to you or the people around you. If a story sounds interesting, take steps to retain it. Don't worry about the source or medium. We tend to avoid use of books, movies and television shows in many settings (especially business) but all of these sources are part of our shared culture.

Start keeping a story journal. Use it to write down your own stories or record other people's stories. A journal doesn't need to be formal. A simple notebook or computer folder works fine. Scrapbooking is another popular form of journaling. It also doesn't matter how you record stories. You may only need a few notes or an outline to remember a story. Or you may prefer to write out a full transcript of the story. You can also keep audio or video recordings of stories.

For each story you record in your journal, include the following elements:

- Theme
- Source
- Format
- Style
- Structure
- Keywords

Use the keywords to suggest situations where the story might work. For example, write down terms such as leadership, management, sales, teamwork, etc. to describe a specific story. The keywords for Tan's Tile might include: "creative thought," "family interaction," "shape patterns," and "Chinese culture."

Matching Stories to Themes

In order to match a story to a theme, follow the SMART Story method. The SMART method helps you match stories to theme based on several parameters: specific, measurable, attainable, relevant and timely. This method is actually derived from the concept of SMART goals often used in business.

Specific

Your story should match your theme as specifically as possible. Don't leave it up to your audience to guess or figure out what you're trying to say. This is common in literature, but not applicable in a business or even a social setting. So-called "teaser" campaigns often just leave the audience dazed and confused. Also, most products tend to fall short of the hype.

Volkswagon recently ran a multi-tiered campaign featuring an old-style bug making speeches. These ads were followed up by the same car interviewing "b-list" celebrities. The final product turned out to be a slightly smaller than average sized SUV. (The model looks suspiciously like the crossover class most other manufacturers had already been producing.)

The new car might have been better served by a man at a gas pump alternating his gaze between the smaller car next to him and his SUV stuffed with over-sized cargo. Ironically, the Volkswagon tagline "have your cake and eat it to" would have worked fine here.

Even social situations require a story specific to your theme. For example, communication is the foundation of any strong marriage. Is it really wise to leave an important topic or point up to an interpretive story? Always choose a story that directly relates to your core message, unless your only purpose is to entertain. This may sound restrictive and harsh but it's simply the most effective way to use storytelling in any situation in which you have a set goal in mind.

Examine the characters, though line and acts and scenes within your story and determine whether or not there is a direct correlation between those elements and the theme. The events and dialog should echo the theme. In Tan's Tile, each time Tan makes a shape a member of his family immediately notices the shape and comments on it. Those instances reflect the theme of creative thinking (assuming you accept that a fox or swan is more creative than a square – that's something you need to determine in audience analysis).

As the ultimate test, tell the story to a friend or test audience and ask them to explain the theme of the story back to you. If their explanation matches your target theme then the story is specific.

Measurable

This term may seem odd when used in connection with a story. We think of measurement as something that accompanies a test or process. However, effective storytelling seeks a measurable outcome, even if it's simply audience enjoyment. In mainstream entertainment this is measured by Nielsen ratings or ticket sales. In advertising and marketing, stories are often measured by gross sales. Training uses testing or performance improvement to gauge the effectiveness of a story.

The trick here is deciding what to measure. In some cases it's clear: sell x number of units or score x amount on an exam. However, the question is more difficult when trying to influence, persuade or introduce an idea. In these cases observed behavior is often the only way to measure success. If you use a story about your own childhood to motivate your son to pitch in more around the house, the measure of success is a change in his attitude or increase in a set of specific behaviors. There's no clear call to action in this case (unless there are specific chores involved).

Determine what behaviors demonstrate the intended motivational or attitudinal change. If you use a story to raise moral around the office, benchmark behaviors might include better punctuality, less time off and people simply smiling more.

In addition to defining the behaviors, you must also determine the average number of instances of that behavior occurring prior to the story. How many times per week does your son offer to help out around the house? What is the current tardiness rate at work? How many sick days have employees taken to date? How many smiles can you count around the office in one day? Once you've determined this number you can decide on a target.

Attainable

The fictional detective Harry Callahan once said: "a man's got to know his limitations." The fact is that not every person can successfully tell every story. This is not a reflection of storytelling skill. Every story simply has its own personality. The personality of the story may not reflect your own storytelling personality.

The best political speechwriters are not just good at writing stories but writing stories that reflect the personality of the politician. Have you ever heard a senator who grew up around the beltway talking about the plight of an under-paid waitress or unemployed factor worker? At best it comes off as a trite stump speech. At worst it comes off as patronizing and pandering.

Think of a storyteller as a singer. Every singer has a certain range within the musical scale. A singer can gradually work to improve the size of their range. However, there is generally a natural limit to his or her highest and lowest point. And a singer is always at their best in the heart of their range, the area where they are at their strongest. There are formats and story styles that are at the heart of your storytelling range. You'll always be best at telling these stories.

Only tell stories that are attainable within your personality and storytelling ability. There's a simply test for this. Tell or read the story out loud, preferably in front of a mirror. Did you feel natural and at ease during the story? If not, consider whether it's just a lack of practice or nervousness. If the unnatural feeling does not come from either of these reasons, then the story is most likely beyond your range at this time.

Relevant

Relevancy is often the most challenging aspect of a story to capture. We instinctively know a good story when we hear it and often experience a desire to use that story again. This sometimes causes us to tell a really good story in the wrong situation. In these cases a story intended to be motivation or educational can quickly become simply entertaining. Stories meant only to entertain can seem relevant to many situations. However, more relevant stories are always more entertaining.

There are two keys to recognizing relevancy in a story:

1. The story should clearly contain the theme.
2. Specific aspects of the story reflect the current situation.

This raises the question: Can you adapt a story to apply to a specific theme or situation? The short answer is yes. However, you'll often need to adapt characters, events and dialog to fit the theme. As you do so, you may negatively affect the through line of the story. Almost any story can be stretched but only up to a certain point. Stick to changes that amount more to embellishment or emphasis of the existing elements.

Timely

There are a number of aspects to consider when judging the "timeliness" of a story. The first is physical: do you have sufficient to time to tell the story in an effective way? Just as many stories can be adapted to be more relevant, they can also be adapted to fit within certain time limits. Good storytellers usually have a short, medium and long version of their stories.

You can generally add and subtract the details of a story to make it longer or shorter – within the original story structure. Switching structures is more difficult though, and not always possible. Have you ever tried to sum up a complicated movie plot in just a few minutes? A narrative cannot always be simplified to an anecdote. Two areas you usually can modify are the level of details (the weather, the location, how the characters looked) and the length of dialog.

The actual timeframe of the story itself also relates to timeliness. A story about a triumphant Roman general may be timely in a motivational speech to the whole company, but not timely in a meeting to plan the company picnic. Here's a general rule to follow: the further the time period of the story is from the current time, the more momentous and serious the occasion must be for the story to be timely.

The third aspect of timeliness is the ability to tell the story at the moment it will have the most effect. The best time to run a car commercial focusing on safety might be right after a news report about a rise in the current accident rate. (Believe it or not advertisers can actually bid on just this type of thing in a show or magazine – or they can even place the story themselves through a press release). The best time for a motivational story at a company is right at the point the company is at the bottom of its current misfortunes.

Unfortunately there's no formula for knowing the "right moment" to tell a story. However, this is a clear case where fortune favors those ready to take advantage of it. The best strategy is to continually find and prepare stories and be ready with an appropriate story when the right moment strikes Of course, there are always times when you will have ample to time to prepare a story, such as a sales pitch or important speech.

Story Sources

The only limit to the number of stories you can find are the number of places you are willing to look. For example, many business people would not consider using a television show episode or movie scene to make a point at work. However, people discuss these topics everyday at the water cooler, coffee machine and lunchroom. Television and movies are an area of shared cultural experience. Not every story has to come from a business book or the Wall Street Journal (although both of these are good sources).

Learn to look for stories anywhere and everywhere. Here is a list of sources to consider:

- Friends
- Family
- Colleagues
- Speakers
- Overheard conversations
- Newspapers
- Magazines
- Books

- Songs
- Plays and Shows
- Legends
- Folktales
- Television shows
- Documentaries
- Movies

Collect the stories you like in your story journal and train yourself to actively look for stories. Discipline yourself to write in your story journal every day. This forces you to discover at least one new story per day. Don't worry about how relevant the story may be to your current situation and challenges. If you think it's a good story, it's probably worth writing down.

Diversion: What Isn't a Story

The artist Andy Warhol pushed the limits of what was and wasn't considered art. His work was part of a larger movement known as deconstructionalism, an offshoot of postmodernism. Deconstructionalism was largely a reaction to the rigid parameters and definitions of the modernist style. It was a way of viewing art and literature in different ways. As a method of study, deconstructionalism can provide fresh insight and new interpretation.

However, deconstructionalism run amuck leads to the expression: "if everything is art, then nothing is art." This has happened to storytelling. It's been asserted that even a corporate speech can be considered a story. Although a corporate speech may contain a story or multiple stories (and probably should to be effective), it is not itself a story or the practice of storytelling. To return to the expression above, if everything is a story, than nothing is a story.

The following items are not stories:

- Non-narrative speeches
- Slogans
- Corporate mission statements
- Reports
- Chronicles or timelines

All of these items generally do not follow any type of storytelling model and do not contain all the necessary elements to make a story. It's also been suggested that's there's something called an "anti-story." Although there is certainly non-traditional and experimental fiction, the notion of anti-story would only exist in a black hole, the

Bizarro Universe or that other dimension they sometimes visit in Star Trek (where everyone wears goatees and sashes.) Either it is a story or it isn't.

When looking for stories, be careful to not be overzealous. Recognize when something is merely an idea and then work with it to turn it into a story.

7 Secrets

- Keeping a story journal is an effective way to find and record stories.
- Match stories to themes using the SMART method: specific, measurable, attainable, relevant and timely.
- Stick with stories that are within your storytelling range.
- Effective stories are always measurable and use a benchmark activity or activities to gauge their return.
- Make sure a story is relevant to the situation and your audience.
- The only limit to the number of stories you can find is the number of places you are willing to look.
- Fortune favors the person who already has the right story for the right moment.

Exercises

Fill in the Blanks

1.A good technique for collecting stories is a
_____ _____.

2. List the six elements of a story you should record:

a. _____

b. _____

c. _____

d. _____

e. _____

f. _____

3. List the five components of the SMART method:

a. _____

b. _____

c. _____

d. _____

e. _____

Discussion Questions

1. What are some story sources you can tap into right away? What are some strategies you can use to collect stories from these sources?

2. What are some ways you can use newer technologies such as the Internet to collect more stories?

Chapter 14 – Putting It All Together

Chapter Objectives

- List the key steps in constructing stories.
- Use the worksheets provided in this book to assist in story creation.

Chapter Overview

This chapter pulls together the information provided in the rest of the book to provide a step-by-step process for creating stories. It also reviews each of the worksheets provided in the book and describes how to use each worksheet to create specific elements of a story.

Introduction

Over the past several chapters, this book has reviewed a number of different components and aspects of storytelling. This chapter offers a step-by-step process to pull all of these elements together in a well-constructed, complete story. The first few times you apply storytelling to practical situations, you should follow the steps closely. Like any other task, though the more you practice storytelling it will eventually become second nature.

Think about the first time you drove a car. You probably had to think about each step and every situation in order to get it right. Now recall the last time you drove to work. How much of the task of driving do you actually remember? Chances are you got to work almost on autopilot. This is known as a unconscious competency: you can perform the task without thinking about it. The more you use storytelling; the more it will become second nature.

Key Steps

It's easier to think of a creating a story as a series of steps designed to construct specific components such as theme, characters and through line. Creating these components is a matter of reviewing elements such as the goal, audience and environment. Use the following steps to pull your stories together:

1. Analyze the situation.
2. Determine the specific goal.
3. Brainstorm story ideas.
4. Choose the most appropriate story.
5. Adapt the story to the goal and situation.
6. Construct the story.
7. Check components against goal and situation.

8. Practice the story (written or verbal).
9. Revise as necessary.
10. Deliver the story.

1. Analyze the situation.

- Analyze the current need
- Analyze the audience
- Analyze the environment

2. Determine the specific goal.

- Visualize the end result
- List the desired effects on the audience
- Write a call to action

3. Brainstorm story ideas.

- Review your story journal
- List out several possible ideas
- Bounce ideas off of other people

4. Choose the most appropriate story.

- Match the story with the goal
- Match the story with the theme
- Match the lesson of the story to the end result

5. Adapt the story to the goal and situation.

- Flesh out the details of the story
- List the main points of your message
- Incorporate the main points into story points

6. Construct the story.

- Write the theme
- Develop the characters
- Create the through line

7. Check components against goal and situation.

- Make sure the theme is relevant
- Make sure the characters are intriguing
- Make sure the through line is well constructed

8. Practice the story (written or verbal).

- Read the story out loud
- Try the story out on other people
- Evaluate your performance

9. Revise as necessary.

- Make changes to the characters
- Improve the through line
- Work on your delivery

10. Delivery the story.

- Tell the story
- Engage the audience
- Evaluate the results

Worksheets

To complete each of the steps above, use the worksheets provided with this book. They are designed to break storytelling down into smaller, more manageable tasks. These worksheets are also a good remedy for difficulty getting started or "writer's block."

Story Planning Worksheet

This worksheet is designed to help you build a story from the ground up. It presents a series of questions designed to help you clarify key information about your story. We tend to think of stories as purely creative endeavors that in the best of circumstances simply spring from the blank page or the open air. In reality, most stories are carefully planned and meticulously crafted.

If that sounds even more intimidating, think about your favorite past time or hobby: restoring old cars, woodworking, papercraft, photography, scrapbooking, etc. Chances are that pursuit involves special knowledge, skills and a lot of practice. Even playing fantasy football or baseball takes a lot of time and devotion in order to win.

No matter how good you are at your favorite hobby, you must have started with little knowledge or skill. Learning to tell good stories is no different than learning that knowledge or skill. Think of the Story Planning Worksheet as the first "how to" book you read about your hobby or the craftsman who taught you.

The Story Planning Worksheet enables you to complete the first few steps in the story construction process outlined in the last section. It covers theme, audience and the other important elements when planning your story.

Audience Analysis Worksheet

Storytelling is a collaboration between the storyteller and the audience. In order to tell a story effectively you must know your audience. Knowing your audience gives you more confidence when telling your story. Also, the process of learning about your audience often provides inspiration for the story itself.

The characteristics of a story's audience can suggest character traits and plot elements. To tease out these details you'll have to ask a lot of specific questions. All of these questions are provided in the Audience Analysis Worksheet.

You may not have an answer to every question on the list, but you should at least consider each one. Questions that are not relevant to your audience can offer just as much insight.

Story Type Worksheet

One of the most difficult aspects of storytelling is deciding which type of story to tell in a specific situation and/or to a specific audience. The Story Type Worksheet is designed to help you choose this crucial aspect by considering important factors including length, formality and complexity.

One of the questions you might have repeatedly asked while reading this book is: "But what about a simple story? Do I really need to do all these steps and consider all these things every single time I want to tell a story to make a point in a meeting?"

The answer is "no," storytelling isn't always complicated. The Story Type Worksheet is designed to help you determine when a story is complicated and when it isn't complicated. You'll probably only need help with this the first few times. After awhile you'll simply get a feel for the amount of work you need to put into a story.

Story Design Worksheet

The Story Design Worksheet is designed to help you put it all together as indicated in the title of this chapter. It combines all the elements you've created within the other worksheets to produce a detailed plan for your story. The result of this worksheet is not the story itself, but a tool to create the story.

Use your choice of type to determine the length and level of detail in your story design. Add as much or as little detail as necessary. When you feel confident you're ready to construct the story, then you've done enough story design planning to create the story.

Acts and Scenes Worksheet

Use the Acts and Scenes Worksheet once you've developed the theme and basic structure of your story. This worksheet will help you flesh out the details of your story according to the traditional three-act structure. Even if you do not intend to use this model, the structure is a good starting point.

The Acts and Scenes Worksheet will help you organize your thoughts and develop the relationship between each individual scene. The main table in the worksheet is organized according to the linear progression of your story (opening, middle, end). However, you may find it useful to fill in the main plot points first.

Character Development Worksheet

Designing good characters is always a challenge. The Character Development Worksheet is based on the series of questions presented in this book. As you answer each question, look for specific characteristics that can help make the character more identifiable, involving and cause the character to experience growth.

Develop and rework the characters until you have several specific items that make the character identifiable and involving. There should also be two to three main elements that will cause the character to experience growth.

Brainstorming Guide

If you're really stuck, use the last worksheet provided with the book: The Brainstorming Guide. This worksheet provides several methods of brainstorming designed to help you generate ideas for prospective stories. Although it's generally best to adhere to the basic three-act structure, this structure is not the best way to generate ideas.

Brainstorming is an activity without boundaries. It's meant to be a first step in the creative process. You can always refine the results of brainstorming later.

Choose the form of brainstorming that suits you best. If you're a more naturally orderly person, an outline or circle diagram will probably work best for you. If you prefer to work in a more "free-form" style free-writing may work best for you.

Getting Started

There's an old expression that says every long journey begins with a small step. Although a bit cliché, the saying makes a good point. Every story begins with just one word, then a phrase, then a sentence. Eventually you'll discover you've put together a paragraph, a page, a chapter and more.

The blank page can be the most difficult hurdle a prospective storyteller faces. There's a classic view of a writer where he or she sits down at the typewriter and eagerly types the title of their book and their name onto a clean sheet of paper. The writer then pulls out the page and places it at the bottom of what he or she hopes is the first of a large stack of finished pages.

The trouble comes when the writer loads that second page. Now he or she must write that all-important first sentence. This first sentence or story opening stops many writers (and storytellers) in their tracks. A quick search of the Internet turns up volumes of suggestions on breaking through this "writer's block."

However, the best idea is to simply avoid the block altogether. Don't bother to type that title page or even to roll that second blank page into the metaphorical typewriter. Start wherever you'd like.

Although this journey begins with a first step just like any other, it can be any step along the journey. You still have to make all the steps, but they don't necessarily have to be in a certain order.

If you have the end of your story in mind, start there. If you have an interesting character, write out the character description. You'll still have to fill in all the missing pieces as outlined in worksheets included with this book. However, fill them out in the order that works best for you. You get to design the path as well as the destination.

Diversion – Storyteller's Block

A blank page (or screen) is an intimidating sight. This is especially true in cases where you have a situation and need to develop an appropriate story. It's always easier to create a story when the story itself is the inspiration. However, writing a story to fit a theme can be difficult. In many cases you'll find yourself facing every writer's big fear: writer's block.

Here are some suggestions for dealing with those moments when you just don't know what to write next:

- Take a walk
- Meditate
- Try free-writing
- Read for awhile
- Put on some music
- Do a mindless task such as cleaning
- Read over some of your past stories
- Start with the ending or another part of the story (other than the beginning)
- Explain the idea or problem to a pet or inanimate object as an exercise to organize your thoughts
- Talk the idea or the problem out with another person
- Post the idea or problem on a writer's forum and ask for feedback

7 Secrets

- Think of creating stories as a series of steps, rather than an abstract task.
- Construct one component at a time.
- Review key elements such as the goal, audience and environment.
- Each worksheet included with this book is designed to help with a specific aspect of storytelling.
- Use the worksheets included with this book to work through each aspect of story creation.
- You don't necessarily have to take each step in order or create each element in a specific order.
- Never start by typing a title page.

Exercises

Fill in the Blanks

1. List the ten steps in story creation:

a. _____

b. _____

c. _____

d. _____

e. _____

f. _____

g. _____

h. _____

i. _____

j. _____

Discussion Questions

1. How would you go about developing a story in which you had only an ending? What are the advantages of knowing how a story ends before you begin writing it?

2. How would you apply feedback and revisions to the process above?

3. Are any of the steps above more important than the others? Why or why not?

Chapter 15 – Delivering Stories

Chapter Objectives

- List the primary areas of concern when delivering verbal stories.
- Follow the ATTACK strategy for creating effective written stories.

Chapter Overview

This chapter divides storytelling delivery into two types: verbal and written. It provides practical advice for each type of delivery.

There are two primary means of delivering stories: verbal and written. Each has its own disadvantages and advantages. This chapter offers tips and advice for delivering stories in each format.

Verbal Stories

Verbal storytelling is the oldest and most traditional form of storytelling. Nothing compares to simply listening to someone tell a story – especially if they are a gifted orator or storyteller. For a new storyteller this performance can seem overwhelming.

However, verbal storytelling is essentially just a form of public speaking. Public speaking can be mastered through two specific methods: preparation and practice. The more you do of both, the better and more confident you'll be about speaking in public.

It's important to remember that your delivery includes both verbal and non-verbal communication. Non-verbal communication can be 50-90% of your message and includes: voice and diction, tone, volume, rate, appearance, posture, gestures and eye contact.

Voice and diction

A presentation is not only about what you say, but how you say it. The best way to learn the following is listening to good speakers and practice.

Tone

Try to vary your tone when speaking. Put emphasis on key words or parts of your speech. When used properly, variation in tone can not only hold your audience's interest but also drive home your speech's objectives.

Volume

Make sure you speak loud enough to be heard. (Yelling doesn't count.) Speak from your diaphragm. Place your hand just above your stomach but below your rib cage. You should feel a muscle that stretches almost across the width of your body.

This is your diaphragm. Practice speaking with your hand on this muscle. Press the muscle in as you speak. Practice this enough and you should be able to project without yelling.

Rate

The rate at which you speak is also important. Try to keep an even rhythm appropriate for the goal of your presentation and that your audience can follow. More complicated topics may require a slower pace. Sometimes you may want to use a faster pace with a motivation speech.

Appearance

Your overall dress should be conducive to the size and formality of your presentation. If you're unsure what dress is appropriate, just ask. Don't wear anything that may distract your audience from the topic of your speech such as very bright colors or "conversation pieces."

Common mistakes are men who try to "express themselves" with their ties, and woman who wear large or overly apparent pins. Look neat and clean but don't "dress to impress."

Posture

Just like your mother said: stand up straight and don't slouch. Enough said.

Gestures

Gestures can emphasis points within your speech. Simple hand gestures add a human touch. However, be careful not to over gesture. If necessary give your hands "something to do" during your speech, such as resting them on a podium or table, or returning them to the "steeple" position (see tip below). Practicing in front of a mirror or on video can help.

Eye contact

It sounds basic, but it's important to look at your audience, and all parts of your audience. Be careful not to simply read from your notes, or worse, read from slides (which turns your back to the audience). The general rule is 3-5 seconds in one place. Once again, practice, practice, practice.

Written Stories

Filling a blank page is a challenge. Filling a blank page with good writing is an even larger one. Good writing is built on four main principles:

1. An understanding of basic grammatical rules and practices.
2. A multi-stage process (plan, organize, write, edit, rewrite).
3. Strategies that improve the product.
4. Continual improvement through writing and reading.

To strengthen your writing, use the following "ATTACK" strategies:

- (A)ctive voice
- (T)rim
- (T)ransitions
- (A)void jargon
- (C)risp
- (K)ey words

Active voice

The spell and grammar checker in Microsoft Word will flag any sentence written in passive voice --and rightly so. Use active voice in almost every situation. Active voice states meaning, assigns responsibility or calls to action.

Trim

You can make your writing more concise by eliminating or "trimming" unnecessary words, including adverbs (quickly, very), introductory phrases ("in the long run"), and word extensions ("try out" instead of "try"). You should also avoid overly long sentences and unnecessarily repetitive sentences.

Transitions

Improve the flow and pace of your writing through transitions. Imagine your sentences as Lego blocks. Although they may come in different sizes and shapes, they must "snap" into each other at multiple points.

The corresponding tips and grooves on Legos represent the ideas within your sentences. They must "connect" on a thematic level. Some methods of creating good transitions include referencing, synonyms and logical relationships.

Avoid Jargon

Always write in language that is clean and easy to understand:

Do:

Use common words - Given the choice between a common and uncommon word that mean the same, use the more common one. Use uncommon words only if they express an idea unique to that word. An example would be "juxtaposed." There isn't a common word that precisely describes relationships in the way this word does.

Use a conversational tone - Try to write in a conversation tone when you can. Pattern your writing after human speech by reading it a lot to see how it sounds. Good writing can be read aloud as an effective talk or lecture. However, balance conversational tone with the required formality of the piece.

Don't:

Use technical terms - Avoid the use of technical or industry-specific terms, especially for their own sake. If you do need to use technical or industry-specific terms, revisit your audience analysis to make a determination whether or not they will understand the term. If not, define it within the piece in a footnote or glossary.

Use "buzz" words – Buzzwords are actually the technical jargon of the business world. Don't use any word that doesn't have clear meaning. If you're unsure, run it up the flagpole and see if anyone salutes. (Just kidding.)

Crisp

Keeping your writing crisp means to write as specific as you can, without giving too much information. The best way to test whether or not sentences are crisp is to simply read them aloud. Crisp sentences flow off the tongue evenly and easily - without the need to take extra breaths or unnatural pauses.

Key words

English sentences are read from left to right. Therefore the reader sees the subject of the sentence first. For this reason sentences that begin with words such as "it" or "there" are inherently weaker than sentences that begin with a noun. Similarly, action verbs such as "develop," "achieve," "build," etc. are stronger than verbs of being such as "is."

Diversion: Simple Meditation

Simple meditation can be a good way to relax and gain focus before telling a story. It can also help you gather your thoughts and overcome writer's block when creating stories. Here are some basic techniques you can use to apply meditation in just a few minutes.

I. Breath and count

1. Inhale deeply.
2. Mentally count "inhale one."
3. As you count avoid intruding thoughts.
4. Exhale and repeat.

II. Simple chant

1. Sit in a comfortable, upright position.
2. Place your thumbs and forefingers together.
3. Focus on a one or two syllable word such as OM, AUM or AMEN.
4. Picture the word in your mind.
5. Whisper the word repeatedly, rhythmically if possible.

III. Flame meditation

1. In a darkened room, light a small candle.
2. Position yourself 10-15 inches away.
3. Stare at the flame intently for 1-2 minutes.
4. Abruptly blow the candle out and close your eyes.
5. Maintain the image of the flame in your mind as long as possible.

7 Secrets

- There are two primary means of delivering stories: verbal and written, each has its own disadvantages and advantages.
- Verbal storytelling is the oldest and most traditional form of storytelling.
- Non-verbal communication can be 50-90% of your message and includes: voice and diction, tone, volume, rate, appearance, posture, gestures and eye contact.
- Good writing requires an understanding of basic grammatical rules and practices.
- Writing is a multi-stage process that includes plan, organize, write, edit and rewrite.
- To increase the quality of your writing, follow the ATTACK strategy: active voice, trim, transition, avoid jargon, crisp and keywords.
- The best way to improve both your verbal and written storytelling skills is practice.

Exercises

Fill in the Blanks

1. List at least five elements of non-verbal communication:

a. _____

b. _____

c. _____

d. _____

e. _____

2. List four of the ATTACK strategies for good writing:

a. _____

b. _____

c. _____

d. _____

Discussion Questions

1. How can you improve your storytelling skills?

2. What opportunities will you have to incorporate storytelling?

Appendixes

Appendix A – Select Glossary

Acronym – A word or short phrase used as a memory device. Each letter in the word or phrase is the first letter of a word in a list or series. Example: BEARS (background, ethnicity, age, relationships and skills in audience analysis).

Action – The core unit within a learning or sales objective. Using an action verb such as "describe," "list" or "explain" to make the objective more measurable.

Action words – Words that specifically describe the act of doing something (as opposed to a "state of being"). Action words make training and ad copy more effective. Examples: "improve," "gain" and "save."

Active voice – Occurs when the verb in a sentence describes the action a subject is taking upon something else (as opposed to passive voice, in which the subject is being acted upon).

Acts and scenes – Basic units within a story, used to break the content into smaller bits. Other terms such as "chapter," "module" and "section" are sometimes used to describe acts and scenes.

Affect behavior – The behavior you are trying to induce or change through your message.

Age – A unit of demographic measurement, it represents the physical age of audience members. It is usually expressed as a range.

Animated characters – Fictional characters sometimes used in training and sales programs that express movement and/or gestures.

Attention – The state in which your audience is actively listening (not just physically hearing) your message.

Association – A memory device that establishes a link between an abstract concept and a definition or skill point. Example: "Take a bite out of crime." The audience associates the dog character and "bite" with combating crime and a neighborhood watch.

Audience analysis – The process of examining an audience to determine key demographics and psychographics including background, ethnicity, age, relationships and skills.

Background – A measurement in audience analysis, describing demographics such as geography, setting, learning style, etc.

Back panel – The side of a brochure or mailing directly opposite the front when the paper is folded. The back panel usually contains non-essential or repetitive information since it is separated by the fold from the rest of the content.

BEARS – Acronym representing the main components of audience analysis within the storytelling method: background, ethnicity, age, relationships and skills.

Bits – A general term describing the idea of breaking content down into smaller and smaller units of information that the audience can comprehend. Humans process information in bits of three to five, and never more than seven.

Bold – Printing a word in heavier type to increase the contrast between it and the other words on a page.

Brainstorm – Developing and considering ideas for a program without a specific goal.

Brand – The consistent perception, vision or "personality" a company projects for itself or its products or services.

Branding – The action of consistently projecting an organization's brand throughout a message and across multiple messages. Branding can also be used as through line.

Bullet point – Offsetting a word, sentence or phrase in print by indenting it and placing a small symbol such as a circle to the left of it.

Chapter – A unit of measurement within a training program or book, containing its own three to five objectives.

Characters – People or metaphorical objects in a story with which the audience can identify. The audience can also be a character in the story.

Circle diagram – A method of brainstorming in which key points are placed inside circles and surrounded by sub-points. Circles and sub-points are then interconnected with lines.

Cognitive challenges – There are three specific cognitive challenges facing you when you deliver a message: attract attention, achieve retention, and affect behavior.

Complexity – Measures the relative difficulty of the content in a story.

Cones – The cone-shaped photosensitive receptor cells of the retina that function in color vision.

Condition – One of the three key components in objectives, conditions describe the pre-requisites that must occur or be present for the objective to be fulfilled. Example: "After completing this training book, you will be able to..."

Contact panel – The panel of a brochure or mailing that contains the "call to action" and the information needed to contact the organization such as website, email, phone, fax, and/or address.

Contrast – The distinction between colors perceived by our eyes and used by our brain to interpret patterns.

Cornea - The transparent part of the coat of the eyeball that covers the iris and pupil and admits light to the interior.

Cost-prohibitive – The point at which a technique, method or program ceases to produce benefits that equal or out weigh its costs.

Distracting elements – Any element in a message that does not directly relate or promote the theme of the message.

Economy of scale – The action of combining repeated actions or items at one time to reduce costs.

Ethnicity – A measurement of audience analysis that describes the cultural background of the audience.

Fable – A legendary story, often containing elements of the supernatural and delivering a moral or message.

Flavor – Describes the style of a story or message.

Free-write – A brainstorming method in which you write continuously whatever words come to mind on a particular topic.

Genre – Describes a category or type of story. Examples: fable, mystery, scenario, role-play. Often used within the academic world.

Goal – The objective or desired result of a message. The goal is expressed as part of the theme of a story.

Grammatical devices – Describes the family of methods for offsetting and organizing material such as bold, bullet points and italics.

Headline panel – The panel of a brochure or mailing that appears first and on top to the audience when the piece is folded.

Hierarchy of Needs – Developed by Abraham Maslow, the Hierarchy of Needs describes specific layers of need every person must fulfill including food, shelter, security, belonging, love and self-fulfillment. Maslow theorized the lower layers must be acquired before the upper layers.

Icebreaker – An exercise designed to help the audience get to know each other and break out of their existing routine.

Inside panel – The panel or set of panels (when unfolded) in a brochure or mailing that usually contains the bulk of the content.

Interpret – Describes the specific point of view held by an audience about your message.

Interviews – Method of obtaining information about your audience by asking a set of prepared questions and recording the answers.

Job aids – Brief descriptions or sets of instructions for performing a specific task designed to be consulted during the function described.

Journal (Story Journal) – A small notebook or place to record story ideas as they occur.

Juxtaposed – An unexpected combination of words, usually contrasting in meaning to each other.

Keywords – Specific words within the theme used to generate ideas for the project.

Legend – A story sometimes regarded as historical yet not completely probable (usually involving the actions of a hero).

Length – The size of the content to be covered, expressed as hours to deliver the message, or the number of words or pages.

Linear path – The action of following a completely straight path through a message, without flashbacks, asides or tangents.

Long-term memory – The chemical-based area of the brain that stores associations that are compared to incoming patterns for interpretation.

Main idea – Central concept behind a story, expressed as part of the theme.

Measurable – Quality of an objective by which it can be compared against the results of a message to determine if the message has been effective or not.

Metaphor - a figure of speech in which a word or phrase is used in place of another to suggest a likeness or analogy between them. Example: this research is nothing but a blackhole.

Module – A unit of measurement within a training or information program, with its own three to five objectives.

Motivation – An individual audience's desire to begin or change a behavior.

Music – The science or art of ordering tones or sounds in succession, in combination, and in temporal relationships to produce a composition having unity and continuity. Music is also an effective memory device.

Objective – A measurable statement regarding the desired effect of a training, sales or marketing message that contains an action, conditions and standards.

Organizational chart – A method of brainstorming in which you outline topics and subtopics using squares and connecting lines.

Outline – A method of brainstorming and organization in which the information is divided into topics and subtopics and indented using bullets or numbers.

Pattern – A repeated and recognizable set of words or shapes.

Permission – An indication from an audience that you may continue to deliver your message, such as a submission of email, address or reply card.

Perspective - The individual interpretation of a topic or story by an audience.

Parable – A brief, metaphorical story designed to teach a lesson or moral.

Personality – The perception or brand of an organization and/or its products and services.

Progressive learning – Method of training, in which a task is presented step by step. The steps already presented are repeated and before each new step is presented.

Real life example – A specific example within your message that uses an individual occurrence from the audience's frame of reference.

Relationships – A measurement of audience analysis that describes the interactions between audience members and the audience to the presenter.

Research – A method of audience analysis and information design that involves gathering material from a number of sources.

Repetition – Stating a point within a message multiple times in an effort to increase retention.

Retention – Movement of a message to long-term memory.

Retina - The sensory membrane that lines the eye, it is composed of several layers including one containing the rods and cones, and functions as the immediate instrument of vision by receiving the image formed by the lens and converting it into chemical and nervous signals which reach the brain by way of the optic nerve.

Return on investment (ROI) – A measurement that compares the amount of benefit from a program against the overall cost of the program.

Role-playing – Method of training in which participants "act out" or simulate realistic situations.

Rods - The long rod-shaped photosensitive receptors in the retina responsive to faint light.

Sample – A portion of the target audience that demographically represents or mirrors the group as a whole.

Sampling – Segmenting a portion of the audience that demographically represents the group as a whole.

Scope – Accurate assessment of the overall amount of content or work involved in delivering a message.

Short-term memory – Temporary storage of images and patterns in the brain that is electrical and cleaned out each evening during sleep.

Standard – Key component of an objective that clarifies the measurement of whether or not the objective has been met. Example: "increase by 10%."

Skills – A measurement in audience analysis that describes the experience level and education of audience members in relation to the message topic.

Summary – One page description of your message, theme and story.

Scenario-based – Method of training in which participants experience a simulated version of realistic events to practice skills.

Story type – Describes the story according to the structure, purpose and style.

Surveys – Method of audience analysis involving distribution of a prepared set of questions to target audience members and then compiling the responses.

Sustainability limit – The amount of information or content in the story which can be used to transmit before the story is no longer affective.

Synonyms - One of two or more words or expressions of the same language that have the same or nearly the same meaning in some or all senses.

Synopsis – One paragraph description of your message, theme and story.

Tangram – An ancient Chinese puzzle consisting of seven shapes that form a square and can be arranged to form several other animal shapes.

Task-based – Type of training designed and organized around the analysis of actual job function and the individual steps involved.

Target (Target audience) – The group of intended recipients for a message and/or story.

Testimonial – Statement by a role model that specifically endorses a product, service or behavior.

Theme – One sentence (or less) description of the intended message, goal and story idea.

Through line – The narrative or plot that carries the audience through a story. Branding can also be used as a through line.

Transition time – The period of time an audience takes to shift their focus and thought process from normal daily activities to a training session.

Visualization – The act of "seeing" an intended behavior in one's mind before the action is actually committed.

Welcome activity (Icebreaker) – An exercise performed at the beginning of a meeting designed to help the audience get to know each other and break out of their existing routine.

Word association – Two different words presented in such a way that the concepts they represent become connected in one's mind. Used as a memory device.

Appendix B – Sample Stories

Baking Bread

This first example story is an excerpt from the book, *The Ginger Bread Man* by Dominic Villari.

"Good dough is the foundation for everything we create," explained the baker. "If the dough isn't right, nothing will work. You must learn to make good dough first."

"How long will it take me to learn to make the dough?" asked Jacob.

"It will take as long as it takes," replied the baker. "Always take the time to learn a skill right."

"Go to the pantry and get the flour, salt and yeast," instructed the baker. Jacob retrieved the items as instructed and placed them on the counter.

"What else do I need?" he Jacob.

"That is all for now," said the baker.

"We're going to make dough from just these three things?" asked Jacob.

"Oh yes," said the baker, "we'll need some warm water."

Jacob went to the facet and ran the water for a few moments until it began to get hotter. "How warm?" he asked.

"Luke warm is fine," said the baker. "Feel your arm."

Jacob felt his arm and turned to the baker. "When it feels as warm as your arm," said the baker, "it's ready."

Jacob brought the water over to other ingredients on the counter. He looked at the baker for further instruction.

"Mix the yeast with the water," instructed the baker.

Jacob mixed the yeast with the water until it dissolved. "Good," said the baker. "Now take some of the flour and make a small mound out of it."

Jacob began to clumsily pile up the flour. The baker shook his head. "You're not concentrating enough," he said.

"It's just a mound," said Jacob. He tried to pile up the flour in random sweeping motions.

"Making dough is deceptively simple," explained the baker. "There are only four ingredients and six steps. But the simplicity makes each of the elements that much more important."

"How can it be simple and complex?" asked Jacob. In his mind he had pictured large mixing bowls, big metal spoons and a vast array of exotic ingredients. He looked down at the lop-sided mound of flour.

"Flour, water, yeast and salt," continued the baker. "The importance of a thing is more than just its complexity and the complexity of a thing is more than just the number of its parts."

Jacob thought about this for a moment. He had always been taught the importance of a job was related to the number of your responsibilities. The more you had to do the more important you must be.

"Who is more important," asked the baker, "the man who does many of the least important jobs or the man who does the few most important jobs?"

"I suppose the second man," said Jacob.

"Making the dough is the most important job," said the baker. "Flour, water, yeast and salt are the most important ingredients."

"I see," said Jacob.

"There are only six steps," continued the baker. "Mix, mound, knead, rise, punch and rise again. But that makes each step very important. Mounding is just as important as rising or kneading."

"I think I understand," said Jacob. He began to shape the flour into a mound again, this time much more deliberately and carefully.

"Good," said the baker. "Do not be distracted; do not rush. Always concentrate on the task at hand as if it is the most important."

"Because in that moment it is the most important," added Jacob.

"That is right," said the baker with a smile. "You are ready for the next step. Make a small pocket in the center of your mound."

Jacob followed the baker's instructions. "Pour in the water?" he asked.

"Yes," replied the baker. Jacob poured the water into the center of mound. "Now place some flour on your hands and begin to knead the dough. Push the dough away with the heels of your hands. Then pick up the opposite edge and fold it toward you."

Jacob tried pushing and folding the dough a couple of times with limited success. "You're rushing again," corrected the baker. "Go slower and concentrate on each move. Push and fold. Push and fold."

Jacob did as the baker instructed and started to maintain a steady rhythm in his kneading. "How long?" he asked.

"What does it matter?" asked the baker.

"But how do I know when it's ready?" asked Jacob.

"When it feels ready," said the baker. "It should be soft and smooth but not too dry. It stops sticking to your hands and springs back to the touch."

"Okay," said Jacob. "If it gets too dry should I add more water?"

"Kneading is about balance," explained the baker. "The right amount of flour, the right amount of water and the right amount of air."

"Air?" asked Jacob.

"Yes," answered the baker. "While you knead you allow air into the dough. The air is food for the yeast and provides a better rise."

The dough felt dry so Jacob added more water. This made it feel too wet so he added more flour.

"Are you feeling with your heart, your head or your hands?" asked the baker.

"My head," said Jacob. "No wait, probably my heart."

"When kneading, feel with your hands," said the baker.

"Oh," said Jacob.

"You'll know when to use your heart and head," said the baker. "For now add a pinch more flour and you should be back in balance."

After around ten minutes the dough started to feel right to Jacob. "I think it's ready," he said and looked at the baker tentatively.

"Good," said the baker. "Shape it into a ball and place it in that bowl. Cover the bowl and allow the dough to rise."

"How long?" asked Jacob. He regretted asking as soon as the words were out of his mouth.

The baker laughed. "Until the dough doubles in size," said the baker. "Probably about two hours."

"I suppose we need to be patient," said Jacob.

"Yes," said the baker. "Or we could make up a batch of sweet dough while we wait."

The Rubber Chicken

The Sacramento Kings are in trouble again. Almost half of their season ticket holders aren't going to renew. This could be financially devastating to a team already on the ropes. The sales department comes up with a well-worded letter about why fans should renew, but they still have a problem.

If ticket holders don't renew, they receive a series of letters from the team. If a fan has already decided not to renew, chances are the letters will go unopened. So the sales department's convincing letter might never even be read.

Then the sales department has another idea. They FedEx the letter to season ticket holders attached to a rubber chicken. The rubber chicken wears a t-shirt with a bad pun.

Wondering what the heck the Kings could be sending them FedEx, all the ticket holders open the package and read the letter. Most renew. Some fans who had already renewed call to see why they didn't get a chicken.

By thinking creatively, the King's sales team manages to differentiate their message.

Kaiser's Ugly Ducklings

Henry J. Kaiser decides he will become a shipbuilder. Never mind his company has never built a ship before. The reality is that America must move millions of tons of cargo to the European war front. Kaiser never considers if it can be done. He only knows it must be done.

Kaiser's first ship takes 244 days to build. She isn't pretty; even the President calls her an "ugly duckling." What she lacks in appearance she makes up for in fortitude. At 442 feet long she moves 10,000 tons of cargo at 11 knots.

By May of 1942, he trims manufacturing time to 72 days. "Building by the mile and chopping by the yard," less than six months later he produces a ship in 46 days. A special team even builds one of the ships in 5 days. A total of over 2700 similar vessels are built and Kaiser builds over a third of them. Liberty ships carry over 75% of all cargo for the war effort.

"I always have to dream up there against the stars. If I don't dream I will make it, I won't even get close." – Henry J. Kaiser. How big are your dreams?

It all started with a refrigerator

People have stopped buying General Electric's refrigerators. It's not that they don't want GE appliances, but the Depression has set in and people just don't have the money. But George Mosher has an idea.

George suggests GE offer customers a way to pay for its appliances over time, a little bit out of each paycheck. Mosher leads the new organization, which lets people buy GE products on credit.

The company is a success and GE Capital, as its called, continues to expand into new areas of credit. The years following WWII bring a change in attitude about financing and the company diversifies into commercial and industrial lending markets.

Today, GE Capital has $66 billion in receivables and employs 90,000 people. They underwrite a variety of lending vehicles including mortgages and department store credit cards. The company even leases airplanes, ships and locomotives.

And it's all because George Mosher was able to think "outside of the refrigerator." Have you thought outside of your organization's refrigerator today?

Dave Thomas

Dave Thomas made a fortune selling hamburgers and chili. He also gave a lot of it away to help others. After working at one of the first Kentucky Fried Chicken locations, Dave started his own restaurant based on the idea of providing hamburgers "the old fashioned way." To Dave that meant using square paddies so more meat was left after cooking and making the burgers to order on a grill.

His formula was successful, and over the years Dave opened thousands of locations across the country. He also pioneered new ideas in the fast food industry such as salads and late night drive through service. Dave still did commercials, even after he'd left everyday management of the company. His warm and casual style made them look as if the camera were simply turned on and he started speaking.

Dave always said whenever he began to doubt his vision; he'd go to the closest Wendy's and order a Single hamburger, small chili and a Frosty. Sampling the company's core products always reassured him.

When was the last time you had a taste of your company's core product?

Teach a man to fish...

Reverend Leon Sullivan, pastor of the Zion Baptist Church in Philadelphia, notices many of the city's business discriminate when hiring workers. He successfully organizes "selective patronage" of several companies and concessions are made. However, the Reverend quickly discovers that those once discriminated against lack the skills to take the jobs now offered.

Reverend Sullivan organizes programs to train the workers and they are able to perform jobs at the now integrated local businesses. "Integration without education equals frustration." Building off this success, Reverend Sullivan starts many programs on the principle that if you give a man a fish, he'll eat for a day. If you teach him to fish, he'll eat for the rest of his life.

Reverend Sullivan's organization, the Opportunities Industrialization Centers and its programs expand across the nation and eventually to the African continent and Poland. His legacy is one of "self help."

Do you give your clients a fish, or teach them to fish?

It's a long way down

It's a long way down. Sir Earnest Shackleton stares at the slope. It's getting colder by the minute, with only an hour or two of daylight left. If the men are too high when the sun goes down, they will surely freeze to death. However, the mountain's sheerness has thwarted their attempts to descend it.

Two days ago they had landed on Seal Island to seek refuge for their stunted expedition. They planned to cross Antarctica, but their ship became trapped in ice.

Forced to abandon ship, they made their way across the ice and through open water to Seal Island. However, they landed on the wrong side. Shackleton decided he and two others would cross the mountains to reach the whaling station. He would then return to save the rest of his men.

Now they may be as doomed as their ship. As Shackleton ponders, he looses his footing and slides several feet down the slope. This gives him an idea. Taking a chance, he has the men form a human toboggan. Sliding, they cover over a thousand feet in minutes. The next day Shackleton and his men reach the whaling station and arrange for a rescue ship.

Robertson's Futility

"She was the largest craft afloat and the greatest of the works of men," Morgan Robertson reads from the paper in front of him. He breathes a sigh of contentment over his opening sentence. Robertson forces himself to take pause, preventing his thoughts from running too far ahead of him. Though he's only begun writing, he can see the entire novel and its subject in his mind.

The ship is 800 feet long and carries over 2,000 passengers across the water at 24 knots. To Robertson, the ship he envisions is both a triumph of human engineering and a statement of man's folly. Her creators claim the ship is unsinkable, but Robertson's narrative holds another destiny.

In Robertson's book, the *Titan* will sail into infamy when she takes damage on her starboard side and sinks. As an extra irony in his story, Robertson plans to deprive the ship of enough lifeboats. The detail symbolizes the ego of the ship's creators and operators.

As Robertson continues writing, he doesn't know that fourteen years later a ship much like the one in his story will experience the same fate, pointing out the same triumph and folly.

What's in a Gardenburger?

"We paid this for one commercial?" ponders the accounts payable clerk. "What are the guys upstairs thinking, anyway?"

The year is 1998 and Gardenburger has just forked over $1.5 million to NBC to air one commercial on the season finale of *Seinfeld*. That's almost half of the company's total budget for advertising. It's a gamble, but the marketing department is hoping the event will help propel the company's products more into the mainstream. And they don't want to wait for the Superbowl.

However, the idea of a company like Gardenburger paying so much for a commercial becomes news in itself. Gardenburger enjoys a wave of publicity long before the ad ever airs, and the commercial itself is almost anti-climatic. Awareness of the product is raised to a degree that sales for the fiscal year double. Gardenburger's market share goes from thirty to over fifty percent.

Sometimes the big gamble pays off, and sometimes it's the indirect consequences of the idea that count.

A lesson at the airport

Dan glances at his watch and looks at the line in front of him. Despite his dash to the airline check-in counter, seven people are ahead of him. His flight to

Boston has been cancelled and he has to see if he could get re-routed. Most of the people in front of him grumble among themselves, getting each other more riled up as they approached the counter. Nearly all of them are terse to the man working behind it. Two people actually yell at the man, who rubs his temples often.

Dan concentrates on his breathing. He counts off each breath as he exhales and starts worrying less about his current situation. By the time he reaches the counter he's calmer. He greets the man at the ticket counter with a smile and a hello. Dan explains his situation and asks if the man can help. The man at the counter taps on his computer for a moment, and manages to re-route Dan on a flight going through Chicago. Dan thanks the man and wishes him a good day. The man behind the counter returns the sentiment and Dan heads off to catch his new flight.

Appendix C – Exercise Answers

Chapter 1

1. Tangram

Chapter 2

1. Attract attention, achieve retention, affect behavior
2. Light
3. Rod, cones
4. Contrast
5. Uncommon patterns

Chapter 3

1. Son
2. Electrical
3. Chemical
4. Long-term memory
5. Association, patterns

Chapter 4

1. Objectives
2. Actions, conditions, standards
3. Unpredictable
4. Foundation
5. Acceptable

Chapter 5

1. Anecdote, episode, narrative
2. Entertaining
3. Approach

4. Historical, journalistic, mythical
5. Structure, purpose, style

Chapter 6

1. Theme
2. Goal, main idea
3. Brainstorming
4. Outline, free-write, research, word association, circle-diagram, organizational chart

Chapter 7

1. Audience analysis
2. Background, ethnicity, age, relationships, skills
3. Research, interviews, surveys, welcome activity
4. Research
5. Formality, length, complexity

Chapter 8

1. Identifiable, involving, growth
2. Invent a character backstory, determine the core values, describe a pivotal moment, compare / contrast to yourself, review relationships, list special skills, list weaknesses, describe potential improvement, explain the importance, list potential interaction points

Chapter 9

1. Plot-driven, character-driven
2. Plot-driven
3. Character-driven
4. Length, formality, importance
5. Balance

Chapter 10

1. Beginning, middle, end
2. Series of lessons through failures, period of growth overcoming challenges, combination of the two
3. Reversal, repetition, resolution
4. Physical, structural
5. Practice

Chapter 11

This exercise contains only discussion questions. For feedback, email us at:
discussion@practicalstorytelling.com.
Place the discussion question in the heading.

Chapter 12

1. Physical conditions, current events, overall atmosphere
2. Describe the situation, determine the possible impact, acknowledge the situation, connect the situation to the theme
3. Theme

Chapter 13

1. Story journal
2. Theme, source, format, style, structure, keywords
3. Specific, measurable, attainable, relevant, timely

Chapter 14

1. Analyze the situation, determine the specific goal, brainstorm story ideas, choose the most appropriate story, adapt the story to the goal and situation, construct the story, check each component against the goal and situation, practice the story, revise as necessary, deliver the story

Chapter 15

1. Voice and diction, tone, volume, rate, appearance, posture, gestures, eye contact
2. Active voice, trim, transitions, avoid jargon, crisp, keywords

Discussion Questions

For feedback on Discussion Questions, email us at discussion@practicalstorytelling.com. Place the discussion question in the heading of the email.

Appendix D – Worksheets

Visit www.practicalstorytelling.com for full size, 8x11″ PDF versions of each of the worksheets in this section. For completed examples of each worksheet, review Chapter XX or visit the website.

Story Planning Worksheet

Instructions

This worksheet is designed to help you develop the core idea for your story using the three principles of attract attention, achieve retention and affect behavior presented in Part I of this book. When planning a story with a specific goal in mind it's best to work backwards from affecting behavior.

Section I – Theme Planning

The first step in developing your story is come up with a clear and concise theme. You should be able to state the theme in one complete sentence.

1. What is the goal of this story?

2. Who is the audience of the story?

3. How much time do you have to tell story?

4. What are some keywords associated with the story?

Use your answers to the questions above to state theme in one sentence. Revise as necessary:

Story name:	
Occasion:	
Theme:	

Keep your theme in mind when considering each of the remaining sections in this worksheet. The rest of the sections are designed around the ideas of attract attention, achieve retention and affect behavior presented in the book.

Section II – Affect Behavior

In this section you'll develop a clear and specific goal for the story by defining the objective(s). Meaningful objectives contain three major elements: actions, conditions and standards.

1. What is the distribution method or venue for the story? (After completing)

2. What do you want the audience to do or be able to do after listening to the story? (Action)

3. What resources will the audience need to complete the Action above? (Conditions)

4. What will be used to determine the success of the Action above? (Standards)

Repeat questions 2-4 until you have listed every goal or objective for your story. Note: If you have more than five goals you may need to use more than one story. Construct your objectives using the answers to the questions above:

After listening to this story, the audience will:

- **Objective A**

    o Conditions:
    o Actions:
    o Standards:

- **Objective B**

  - Conditions:
  - Actions:
  - Standards:

- **Objective C**

  - Conditions:
  - Actions:
  - Standards:

Section III – Achieve Retention

In this section you'll use the objectives you developed in Section II to brainstorm Examples and Metaphors to embed in your story.

Consider the following questions for each of the objectives you outlined in Section II.

1. What are some examples of how you've seen this objective in practice (real or imagined)? What stories contain examples of this objective?

2. What are some metaphors or ways of illustrating this objective? What other actions in life does this objective resemble?

	Examples	Metaphors
Obj. 1		
Obj. 2		
Obj. 3		

Repeat questions 1-2 for each of the objectives you identified above. Hint: Use a separate sheet to brainstorm ideas or complete the Brainstorming Worksheet for each objective.

Section IV – Attract Attention

In this section you'll identify the best examples and metaphors from Section III and expand them out into ideas to incorporate into the story. These ideas provide the uncommon patterns that will make your story attract attention and form the backbone of the through line.

1. Read through the examples and metaphors in Section III and circle the best two or three from each objective. (For a shorter story such as anecdote you may only need one example or metaphor for each objective.)

2. For each of the ideas you identified, answer the following questions: How does the idea relate to the theme? How can you use the idea to demonstrate the theme? What can the idea teach us about the characters? How can the idea move the through line forward? How can you relate the idea to the audience? What is the beginning, middle and end of the idea?

Idea 1	Metaphor/Example:
	Expand:
Idea 2	Metaphor/Example:

Idea 3	Expand:
	Metaphor/Example:
	Expand:

Idea 4	Metaphor/Example:
	Expand:
Idea 5	Metaphor/Example:
	Expand:

Idea 6	Metaphor / Example:	
	Expand:	
Idea 7	Metaphor / Example:	
	Expand:	

Repeat the steps above for each of the best ideas you identified in Section III. During this process you may find some of the ideas don't work as well as you initially thought. Replace these ideas with others from your initial list or come up with new ideas to replace them. As you expand each of the ideas, they may suggest other examples and metaphors.

Audience Analysis Worksheet

Section I – Basic Analysis

Use the questions below to analyze your audience. Then summarize your findings in the Analysis table after the questions. Include in your analysis any ideas, concerns or ideals the audience may hold based on their characteristics.

Audience Analysis Questions

Background

1. What is the geographic location(s) of the audience?

2. What is the specific setting (or channel) in which you'll deliver your message?

3. Is the audience familiar and/or comfortable with this setting?

4. What percentage of your audience is male? Female?

5. Is your audience liberal or conservative?

6. What is the general personality of your audience?

7. Has the audience heard your message or messages from you before?

8. How participatory or non-participatory is your audience?

9. Is the presentation of your message required or voluntary?

10. What other messages is the audience receiving (besides yours) during the time you'll be delivering your message?

Ethnicity

1. Does the audience use English as a second language?

2. How many years of experience speaking and writing English does your audience have?

3. Are there euphuisms and metaphors the audience will not understand?

4. What are some of the major cultural features of the audience?

5. Are there specific traditions or examples that can be used in your message?

6. What are the traditional educational or training roles in the audience's culture?

7. Are there culture-related topics or examples you should avoid?

8. Does your audience contain a mix of cultures?

9. Are there cultural examples that can be shared by the entire audience?

10. How does your cultural background relate to the audience?

Age

1. What is the age range of your audience?

2. What is the average age?

3. How are ages distributed throughout the audience?

4. How do the age ranges within your audience relate to each other?

5. What generations are represented in your audience?

6. Are there specific values, traditions and/or ideals within the age groups?

7. Are there specific traditions or shared experiences in your audience's age group(s) that you can use to convey your topic?

8. How does the topic relate to the specific age groups in your audience?

9. How does the age of your audience compare to your age?

10. How do the age ranges in your audience compare to each other?

Relationships

1. Do the members of your audience know each other?

2. Are the members of your audience from a specific organization or trade?

3. Are there specific examples that speak directly to this particular group?

4. Do the members of your audience represent different levels of influence?

5. Are there both managers and employees in your audience?

6. Is everyone in your audience a decision-maker and/or influencers?

7. What is the audience's relationship to you?

8. Does trust exist between you and the audience?

9. Does the audience have more or less experience than you?

10. How does the audience's occupation and position relate to yours (higher or lower)?

Skills

1. What is the skill level of the audience in relation to your topic?

2. Does the audience understand the technical vocabulary regarding your message?

3. Is your topic completely new to the audience?

4. Is your message a specialized area within a topic the audience already understands?

5. What is the educational level of your audience?

6. How does the educational level compare to yours?

7. How does the audience's level of knowledge about the topic compare to yours?

8. How many years of experience does the audience have in the topic or topic area?

9. Is there information on the topic your audience can offer you?

10. Are there other skills that will help the audience relate to your topic?

Audience Analysis Table	
Background	
Ethnicity	
Age	
Relationships	
Skills	

Section II – Perspective, Concerns and Benefits

In this section you'll use the information above to list out the audience's perspective, concerns and benefits on the theme of your story. You will also develop strategies to deal with each perspective and concern. For a longer story, break your theme down to smaller components or individual topics and fill out a table for each component or topic.

Theme:	
Benefits	Use this area to list the specific ways the audience can benefit from the theme of your story. Use these benefits when developing strategies to overcome the perspectives and concerns below.
1.	
2.	
3.	
4.	
Perspective	**Strategy**
Use this area to list any ways in which the audience's ideas or ideals influence the way they may interpret the story.	Describe a strategy you can use to overcome the perspective.

Concern	**Strategy**
Use this area to list any specific concerns or problems the audience may have regarding the theme of the story.	Describe a strategy you can use to overcome the perspective.

Story Type Worksheet

This worksheet is designed to help you determine and develop your story type. Remember that story type encompasses three main components: structure, purpose and style. However, the first step is to rate your topic in terms of length, formality and complexity. Use this information to pick out an appropriate structure, purpose and style using the descriptions of each of these elements presented in the book.

Length

Determine your length by examining the number of pages or words if your story delivery is written or by time to present if your story is oral.

Pages / Words of Content: ____   x   (.10 or .25)
= Story length: ____

Hours to present material: ____   x   (.10 or .25)
= Story length: ____

Formality

Audience Formality		Guidelines: Age, conservative, professional		
1	2	3	4	5
Min.		Avg.		Max
Topic Formality		Guidelines: Criticalness, legality, safety		
1	2	3	4	5
Min.		Avg.		Max.

Complexity

Topic Complexity		Guidelines: Skill level, experience, overall size		
1	2	3	4	5
Min.		Avg.		Max.

Use the length, formality and complexity to choose an appropriate structure, purpose and style based on the descriptions provided in the book. After choosing a possible story type, develop the first couple of pages or few minutes of the story. Read this small section aloud and compare again against your ratings on this sheet. If the story type still appears correct, develop the rest of the story. If it does not, choose a new story type and repeat the process.

Story Design Worksheet

Collect all the other worksheets you've completed and summarize the main points on the following worksheet. This worksheet serves as an overview for your story. Use this worksheet as a review activity before starting the main work on your story. You may also want to read over this sheet again before you deliver the story.

	Description	Source
Theme	One sentence statement of the goal and main idea behind the story.	Story Planning Worksheet (Sec. I)
Summary:		
Audience Analysis	Summary of the perspective, concerns and benefits of the audience.	Audience Analysis Worksheet
Summary:		
Through line	Bulleted timeline of the story's major events or elements.	Act and Scene Worksheet
Summary:		

Characters	One sentence description of each of the main characters in the story.	Character Design Worksheet
Summary:		
Acts and Scenes	Outline containing the content of the story.	Act and Scene Worksheet
Summary:		

Act and Scenes Worksheet

This worksheet is designed to help you divide your story into smaller, manageable pieces. The end result is a "roadmap" you can follow when writing or developing the full story. This worksheet is based on the idea that humans digest information in bits of three to five and never more than seven.

The worksheet is built around the traditional three-act structure used in many books, movies and televisions shows. Although you are free to experiment with different structures, the three act model is a good starting point.

The table below breaks the three act structure down to its main components. The pivotal components in each act are the Opening, Plot Point and Resolution (Act 3). Fill these areas in first – they are the most important areas of your story. After you have completed these components, fill in the content areas in each act using the balance and rhythm guidelines described in Chapter 10. Use the Story Development Questions on the next page to help you fill out each section.

ACT 1		
Opening		
Content		
Plot Point		

ACT 2		
Opening		
Content		
Plot Point		

ACT 3		
Opening		
Content		
Plot Point		

Story Development Questions

Opening

1. How does the opening catch attention?

2. What immediate impression do we have of the characters?

3. How does the opening set the stage for future events?

Content

1. What events take place during this content section?

2. What dialog or conversation takes place during this content section?

3. How does the content build upon the opening of the act?

4. How does this content section resolve the previous plot point?

5. How does the content build towards the next plot point at the end of the act?

6. How does the content demonstrate the traits of the main characters?

7. What do the characters gain in the scenes within the content?

8. What do the characters lose in the scenes within the content?

9. How does the content in this section foreshadow or set up events in future sections?

10. What lessons do the characters learn during this content section?

Plot Point

1. What pivotal event occurs at this plot point?

2. How does this plot point change the course of the story?

3. How do the characters react to this plot point?

Resolution

1. How are all the "lose ends" tied up?

2. In what ways do we clearly see growth or change in the main characters?

3. How does the resolution remind the audience of the theme?

Character Development Worksheet

Compelling characters are identifiable, involving and experience growth. This worksheet is designed to help you develop effective characters according to these guidelines. Answer each of the questions below. Use the first column to brainstorm ideas. Adapt your ideas into a list of ways the character can be identifiable, involving and experience growth in the remaining three columns. (Not every question need provide results in all the columns.)

Brainstorming	Identifiable	Involving	Growth
What is the backstory of the character?			
What are the values of the character?			
Describe a key moment in the character's life.			
How is the character similar to you? How is the character different from you?			
What are the character's relationships with the other characters in the story?			

Brainstorming	Identifiable	Involving	Growth
What are the character's special skills?			
What are the character's weaknesses?			
What are some ways this character can grow?			
Why is this character important?			
In what ways will this character interact with the other characters?			

Brainstorming Guide

This guide provides an example of each brainstorming type previously described. The example used in each is the book itself. You should recognize many of the concepts and ideas. Notice how they come together differently depending on the specific brainstorming method. Each is equally affective, though.

Outline

A. Overview

       1. Opening story
       2. Attract attention
       3. Achieve retention
       4. Affect behavior

B. Application

       1. Theme
       2. Audience analysis
       3. Story types

Circle Diagram

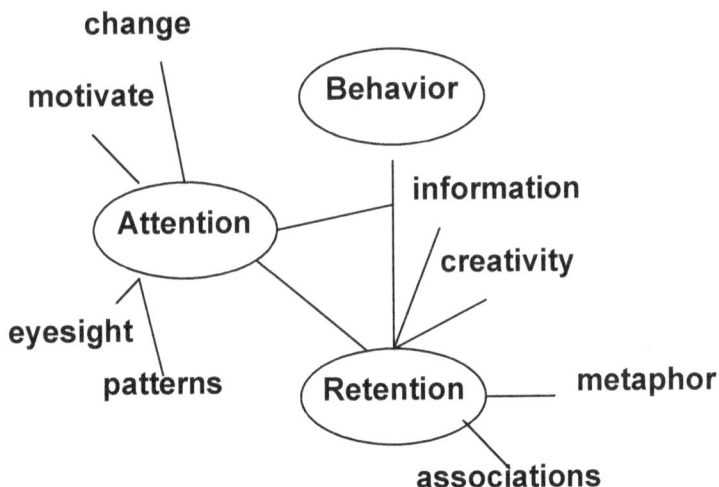

change

motivate

Behavior

Attention

information

creativity

eyesight

patterns

Retention — metaphor

associations

Free-write

Stories attract attention through uncommon patterns. Achieve retention through associations and pattern – metaphors. Brainstorming. Derive central idea – construct theme. Theme central element. Theme planning worksheet. Audience analysis: BEARS. Tie analysis to through line and story type. Use story for entire course – demonstrate storytelling within lessons. Decontruct central story...

Word Association

Word: Story
Associations: Tale, narrative, thorugh line, plot, characters, metaphors, scenario

Word: Audience
Associations: Demographics, geography, psychographics, survey, research, poling, questions

Research

Attract attention

- Eyesight, use of rods and cones to refract light; image examined by brain (source: see weblinks)
- Long-term (chemical), short-term (electrical) memory (source: Williams)
- Hiearchy of Needs (Maslow)

Organizational Diagram

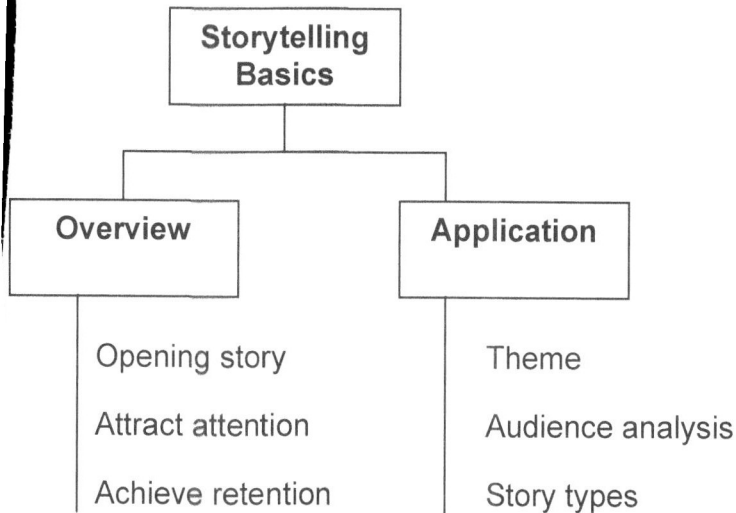

```
        ┌──────────────┐
        │ Storytelling │
        │   Basics     │
        └──────┬───────┘
        ┌──────┴───────┐
  ┌─────┴────┐    ┌────┴────────┐
  │ Overview │    │ Application │
  └─────┬────┘    └────┬────────┘
        │              │
  Opening story      Theme

  Attract attention  Audience analysis

  Achieve retention  Story types
```

www.ingramcontent.com/pod-product-compliance
Lightning Source LLC
Chambersburg PA
CBHW022102280326
41933CB00007B/227